Protégé

Five Things You Should Know About Jesus Christ

New Generation Ministries

The Word of God

Self Awareness ✝ Economic Stability

Community Service

Reaching Our Youth With A Message Of Hope, Deliverance, and Victory !!!

Unless otherwise indicated, all Scriptural quotations will come from the King James Version of the Bible.

Copyright © 1993
Second Edition – First Printing February 2006

Dr. Russell M. Morrow -**Protégé** *Five Things You Should Know About Jesus Christ*
ISBN #0-9776480-9-5

Published by Main Street Publishing, Inc., Jackson, TN.
Copyediting and editing by Amanda Avery.and Annette Galloway
Cover Design by Dr. Russell M. Morrow and Annette Galloway
Printed and bound by NetPub, Poughkeepsie, NY.

For more information write Main Street Publishing, Inc., 206 East Main Street, Suite 207, P.O. Box 696, Jackson, TN 38302. Phone 1-731-427-7379 or toll free
1-866-457-7379. E-mail:words@mspbooks.com for managing editor
and mspsupport@charterinternet.com for customer service.
Visit us at www.mainstreetpublishing.com and www.mspbooks.com.

Learn more about New Generation Ministries - visit www.newgenmin.org

Protégé

Five Things You Should Know About Jesus Christ

by
Dr. Russell M. Morrow

Main Street Publishing, Inc.   Jackson, TN

Protégé

Dedication

This book is dedicated to my wife and children,
Elaine, Chastidy, Audrey, Russell, Jr. and Reginald

And to the loving memory of
my mother and grandmother
Audrey A. Morrow and Mother Helen Cook

Protégé

Table of Contents

Protégé

Introduction

Now is the time to accept Christ in your life

"Don't let the excitement of being young cause you to forget about your creator. Honor Him with your youth before the evil years come when you'll no longer enjoy living.

It will be too late then to try to remember Him, when the sun and moon and stars are dim to your old eyes, and here is no silver lining left among your clouds.

For there will be a time when your limbs will tremble and age, any your strong legs will become weak, and your teeth will be to few to do their work, and there will be blindness.

Then let your lips be tightly closed while eating, when your teeth are gone! And you will waken at dawn with the first note of the birds; but you will be deaf and tuneless, with a quivering voice. You will be afraid of heights and falling, a white-haired, withered old man, dragging himself along: without sexual desire, standing at death's door, and nearing his everlasting home as mourners go along the streets"

Ecclesiastes 12:1-7

Since the beginning of the new millenium, our world has changed drastically as of 9/11. In addition we have been in a war on terrorism, and have had to face the realities of natural disaters such as hurricanes, earthquakes, tsunamis, and even the threat of pandemic outbreaks.

As we face these and other problems in this new millennium, you, the first generation of the new millennium have a tremendous responsibility. You have the responsibility of preparing for and leading our world and bringing about the positive change our society needs.

America's economic, moral, and spiritual decline has fueled the deterioration of the family. Because of the decline of the family, mental illness, drug abuse, alcohol abuse, sex abuse, murder and suicide have destroyed or hindered many of our young people in achieving success.

In talking to teenagers around the country, I have found that many there are so many distractions and pressures that it is hard for many youth to set goals and objectives that will make a difference in their lives and the lives of their love ones. Two distractions are fear and uncertainty about the future. Another distraction is because they are being fooled by the fantasies and false realities of television, movies, videos, drugs, and sex.

Ecclesiastes 12, verse 1-7 tells us that our youthful days will go away quickly. In the 4th chapter of James in verse 14, we are told that live is uncertain, it is like a vapor that appears for a moment and then vanishes. Life is short. It is too short to waste fighting, killing, living in mental, spiritual, and physical poverty.

Because life is so short and many teenagers need a better understanding about life, I will offer you five truthful messages of hope, deliverance and victory rooted in God's Word. These five messages taken from the scriptures will help you get a better understanding about live and the part you play in it. I encourage you to read all of the scriptures referenced in this book because these scriptures serve as a foundation on which you can build a victorious life in Christ I spite for the problems you face everyday.

With these five scriptures you will be able to develop a

clear, realistic and practical understanding of what it meant to have a relevant relationship with Jesus Christ. This is very important because Christ in our lives will make the difference in the future. As you read this book, be confident that God knows that you are dealing with many temptations, challenges, and demands every day for your life. Be confidant that God knows your frustrations, confusions, personal problems, and feelings of hopelessness at this stage in your life. Be confidant that God can and will meet you the point of your needs.

As you read this book I hope that your will receive God's Truth and experience the love, grace, and healing power of God through Jesus Christ in your life. Jesus said in John 8: 31-32: *"If ye continue in my Word you shall know the truth and the truth shall make you free."* Be free my brothers and sisters.

Protégé

Chapter 1

"The thief comes but to steal, kill, and destroy, but I come that you might have life and have it more abundantly." John 10:10

Knowing Jesus Christ as your Lord and Savior is the greatest thing that can happen in your life. This is good news for you as you try to make your way through life's maze, experiencing the pains and realities of growing up, through your teenage and young adult years.

If you ask yourself, "Who or what can offer me the most in life?" You may say, "a complete education so you can get a good job." You may say, "a genuine friend or companion who will love me for who I am and the way I am." You may even say "a professional career that will bring me status, influence, and power." Whatever you believe will give you what you want most in life, remember that Christ has much more to offer you.

Christ's Invitation to You

Because Jesus Christ has more to offer you, he invites you to know him. If you are reading this book and do not know Jesus Christ as your personal Savior, he wants you to get to know him. If you are reading this book and do know Jesus as your personal Savior, he wants you to get to know him better.

Jesus invites you to know him as a personal savior and friend who will go through life with you. Throughout your life, Jesus will help you to adjust, grow in wisdom, knowledge and understanding so that you can live a productive and successful life. Today, Jesus invites you to be his protégé.

Protégé - *Someone who is under the care and protection of an influential person who can help them in their life as it relates to their career or lifestyle.*

In the Bible, Samuel was the protégé of Eli, and Timothy was the protégé of Paul. As a protégé of Jesus you will also learn how to live life in the fullness of God's joy, peace, and prosperity. You will also be a spirit-filled, anointed example who will serve God. You will do so by telling others that are lost, distressed and troubled about the love of Christ and how to meet Him. You will also encourage others who are trying to grow stronger in the Lord.

By accepting Jesus' invitation to be his protégé and learning all about his love and promises, you will give yourself a great advantage in life. You will grow up with the benefit of Jesus being your personal friend, John 15:13-15. Jesus tells us in John 10:10, *"The thief comes but to steal, kill, and destroy, But I come that you may have life and have it more abundantly."*

Jesus wants all that believe on him to live victorious lives. For example, Jesus wants you to have the best grades possible in school and better relationships with your family and your friends. He wants you to have his peace and joy in your life no matter how troubled the world may be. Jesus also wants you to experience true prosperity in your life. This is God's will for you. The thing that will hinder you from achieving the will of God in your life is the influence of sin. Always remember that: SIN ROBS YOU OF GOD'S BLESSINGS.

Webster's Third International Dictionary defines sin as *"an offense against God."* For centuries Satan has been trying to stop people from receiving the best that God has for them. He has done it by influencing the world against Christ and those who follow Christ.

Satan has done it by tempting us to make satisfying our physical passions our highest priority. He has done it by confusing the minds of many people, young and old alike, until they are no longer sure what is right and what is wrong. He has also done it by tempting us with desires for power, influence, control and pleasure.

Although Satan has been trying to stop you from fully knowing and experiencing what God has for you, do not let him get over on you. Do not miss the opportunity of your life to be a part of a new generation of Christians who will live the abundant life. Remember that Satan's desire is to rob you of abundant life but Jesus wants you to have abundant life.

The Bible teaches us that God has provided for us the weapons, tools, and all the power needed to overcome the influences of sin and to achieve abundant life. But we first need to know who our enemies are. In the Bible we can find three spiritual enemies that will hinder us from experiencing abundant life. The Bible also tells us how to defeat these enemies.

Spiritual Enemies

The World: *"You adulterous people, don't you know that friendship with the world is hatred toward God? Anyone who chooses to be a friend of the world becomes an enemy of God."* James 4:4 NIV

Our Flesh: *"For the sinful nature desires what is contrary to the Spirit, and the Spirit what is contrary to the sinful nature. They are in conflict with each other, so that you do not do what you want." Galatians 5:17. NIV*

The devil: *"Be self-controlled and alert. Your enemy the devil prowls around like a roaring lion looking for someone to devour." I Peter 5:8 NIV*

Overcoming the Enemy

The World: *"Do not conform any longer to the pattern of this world, but be transformed by the renewing of your mind. Then you will be able to test and approve what God's will is—his good, pleasing and perfect will." Romans 12:2*

Our Flesh: *" So I say, live by the Spirit, and you will not gratify the desires of the sinful nature." Galatians 5:16.*

The devil: *"Submit yourselves, then, to God. Resist the devil, and he will flee from you." James 4:7*

Invest in Jesus and be His Protégé

Because Jesus has so much to offer you I encourage you to make an investment today. Invest your life in Jesus. By investing your life in Jesus Christ, whatever endeavor you choose in life will be greatly enhanced. By investing your life in Jesus now you will have a head start on your peers who have not accepted Christ in their life. If you invest your life in Jesus now, you will develop an understanding about life, who you are where you are going, and your purpose in life.

When you know your purpose in life, people cannot intimidate you, make you feel bad with destructive criticism or make you feel insecure. Like the Biblical characters of David, Samuel, Joseph and even little Jesus, you will know your purpose in life and achieve it.

I knew as a child that God gave me a purpose in life, and I believe that God gives all of us a purpose as children. He gives us visions, ideas of what we will be, and what we will do in life. Sometimes when you tell others about your aspirations they might tell you to get real. They might try to discourage you, or they might brush it off as a childhood whim. If you have the desire to be a minister, bank president, a stockbroker, a teacher, or the President of the United States, then go for it.

In the second chapter of Luke there is a very meaningful story about Jesus and how he knew his purpose in life as a preteen. I'll highlight it for you now but make sure you take the time to read it. In this story Jesus traveled with his parents to Jerusalem to the "Feast of the Passover."

When the people from Israel and Judea went to Jerusalem for special events they traveled together in caravans. Somewhat like church or school trips using two or more cars or buses, the difference being they traveled on foot, donkeys, horses and wagons. Do you get the picture? On this particular occasion Jesus was twelve years old when his parents took him to Jerusalem to celebrate the Passover, an occasion which led to Israel's independence from Egypt.

On their return, Jesus did not come back with the caravan. When his parents looked for him and could not find him anywhere in the group they panicked and began a three-day search for Jesus. Their search took them back to Jerusalem where they found Jesus in the temple sitting with doctors, listening and asking questions. When his mother questioned him about leaving the caravan and staying behind, Jesus asked his mother; *"But why did you need to search? Didn't you realize that I would be here at the Temple?" Luke 2:49 (The Living Bible)*

When you read this passage of scripture in its entirety, I want you to be aware of the following things about Jesus. These things make him an excellent role model to pattern your life after. First, Jesus at the age of twelve knew his purpose in life. Second, he began doing something about it. Third, he honored his parents with obedience. Fourth, he grew up having it together mentally, physically, spiritually, socially, while having favor with God and man.

Jesus had it together mentally: Jesus knew the value of learning. He knew how to watch, listen, and think for himself. Jesus could understand what he had learned and had the wisdom to effectively apply this knowledge to fulfill his purpose. Jesus also knew how to adjust so he could live in this world with others.

Jesus had it together physically: Jesus knew the importance of the human body and kept it clean and healthy. Jesus learned the trade of his earthly father Joseph and worked as a carpenter. In his ministry Jesus did much physical exercise by walking. Sometimes Jesus walked distances of over seventy miles from Jerusalem to Galilee. He had to be strong and healthy to speak to great multitudes of three and five thousand people without a public address system. He also had to be physically powerful to turn over the tables of the merchants that dishonored the temple of God. Mark 11:15-17

Jesus was together spiritually: There were three occasions in the New Testament when God gave approval of his work, which shows us the quality of spiritual life Jesus had. The first time was at the Jordan River when John the Baptist baptized Jesus.

"And Jesus, when he was baptized, went up straightway out of the water: and, lo, the heavens were opened unto him, and he saw the Spirit of God descending like a dove, and lighting upon him: And lo a voice from heaven, saying, This is my beloved Son, in whom I am well pleased" Matthew 3:16-17

The second time that God gave his approval of Jesus occurred on the Mount of Transfiguration: *"And after six days Jesus taketh Peter, James, and John his brother, and bringeth them up into a high mountain apart, and was transfigured before them: and his face did shine as the sun, and his raiment was white as the light.*

And behold, there appeared unto them Moses and Elias talking with him. Then answered Peter, and said unto Jesus, Lord, it is good for us to be here: if thou wilt, let us make here three tabernacles; one for thee, and one for Moses, and one for Elias.

While he yet spake, behold, a bright cloud overshadowed them: and behold a voice out of the cloud, which said, 'This is my beloved Son, in whom I am well pleased; hear ye him.' And when the disciples heard it, they fell on their face, and were sorely afraid. And Jesus came and touched them and said, Arise, and be not afraid. And when they had lifted up their eyes, they saw no man, save Jesus only," Matthew 17:1-8

The third time God gave approval of Jesus took place after Jesus made his triumphant entry into Jerusalem on what we celebrate today as Palm Sunday. Jesus, speaking to his disciples said, "... *Now is my soul troubled; and what shall I say? Father, save me from this hour: but for this cause came I unto this hour. Father, glorify thy name.*

Then came a voice from heaven, saying, I have both glorified it, and will glorify it again. The people therefore, that stood by, and heard it, said that it thundered: others said, an angel spoke unto him," John 12:27-29

Jesus had it together socially: Everywhere Jesus went people flocked around him and loved him because he was love in action; he loved God, and he loved his fellowman. Jesus treated people right. The only people that had something against Jesus were the people that felt threatened by his popularity and influence.

As a protégé of Jesus, you too will increase in wisdom, stature, and favor with God and man as you seek to improve yourself. You will improve yourself by reading your Bible, by studying your class work, through discipline, self-control and hard work. All that Jesus had as a teenager is available to you.

By becoming a protégé of Jesus, you can achieve your goals in life with greater wisdom, knowledge, understanding and confidence. Becoming a protégé of Jesus is a wise move for anyone who is thinking about or planning their future. It is also a wise move for every youth who is ready to throw in the towel and give up on life.

As a protégé of Jesus you will grow and learn to know Him through His love, His grace, and His Word. You will also grow and learn to know Him through worship, prayer, fellowship, and devotion. As his protégé, you can learn from Jesus' teachings how to live a life of victory over the influences of sin in the world. By being a protégé of Jesus, you will also learn early how to handle the difficult times in your life.

Jesus is an excellent role model and hero because he lived a fulfilled life, and successful life, and Jesus lived an abundant life. Another reason Jesus is an excellent role model and hero is because he defeated the power of Satan. He defeated Satan on Calvary's cross and in the grave. In Jesus we have a hero whose love is more powerful than all the power and influences in the world.

You can check out the superstars of boxing, football, baseball, basketball, hockey, and wrestling. You can look at superstars in entertainment and motion pictures, but none of them can compare to the greatness of Jesus Christ. They can never thrill you or give you as much joy, peace and contentment as Jesus can. **Jesus is the real deal!**

Here Is What You Should Do

To become a protégé of Jesus you must first trust Jesus Christ and receive his invitation to be saved. To be saved means to come into fellowship with God by accepting Jesus Christ as your Lord and Savior and establishing a personal relationship with Him. Read the following scriptures.

- ◆ *"For God so loved the world that he gave his only begotten son, that whosoever believeth in Him should not perish but have everlasting life," John 3:16.*
- ◆ *"...Repent and be baptized every one of you for the remission of sin and ye shall receive the gift of the Holy Ghost," Acts 2:38.*
- ◆ *"If thou salt confess with your mouth the Lord Jesus and shall believe in thine heart that God raised him from the dead, you shall be saved," Romans 10:9.*
- ◆ *"Behold, I stand at the door and knock. If anyone hears My voice and opens the door, I will come in to him and dine with him, and he with Me," Revelation 3:20.*
- ◆ *"But as many as received Him, to them He gave the right to become children of God even to those who believed on His name," John 1:12.*

If you are looking for someone to believe in and you want fulfillment in your life, accept Jesus in your life right now. Become a protégé of Jesus; it is a good move.

- • Admit your need (I am a Sinner).
- • Be willing to turn from your sins (Repent).
- • Believe that Jesus Christ died for you on the cross and rose from the grave (Faith).
- • Pray and invite Jesus Christ to come in and control your life through the Holy Spirit (Let Christ in your heart).

Pray this Prayer

Dear Lord Jesus,

I know that I am a sinner and need your forgiveness. I believe that You died for my sins and I want to turn from my sins. I invite you to come into my heart and life. I want to trust you as Savior and follow you as Lord, in the fellowship of your Church.

Signature _____ Date _____

Trust God's Word for Assurance

- *"For whoever calls upon the name of the Lord shall be saved," Romans 10:13.*
- *"He who has the Son has life; he who has not the Son has not life. These things have I written to you who believe in the name of the Son of God, that you may know that you have eternal life, and that you may continue to believe in the name of the Son of God," I John 5: 12-13*

Your New Life

By receiving Christ, we are born into the family of God through the supernatural work of the Holy Spirit who dwells in every believer; this is called regeneration or "new birth." This is just the beginning of a wonderful life in Christ. To deepen this relationship you should:

1. Read your Bible every day to get to know Christ better.
2. Talk to God in prayer every day.
3. Tell others about Christ.
4. Worship, fellowship, and serve God in a church where you

will experience good preaching and teaching about Christ.
5. As Christ's ambassador in a needy world, display your new birth through your love and concern for others. (Adopted from a Billy Graham Crusade Tract)

The Blessings

You will realize many wonderful blessings in your life because you received Christ in your life and became his protégé. In this segment I will talk about three specific blessings that come with your salvation through Jesus Christ.

Blessing #1 - You become a new creature. *"Therefore if any man be in Christ Jesus he is a new creature: old things are passed away; behold, all things are become new,"* II Corinthians 5:17.

When you become a new creature in Christ, the Holy Spirit will be your guide and companion. Your life will change reflecting your growth and development in the Lord. In Galatians 5:17-23, the Apostle Paul teaches us that a life without the Holy Spirit will reflect the "Works of the Flesh and that a life with the Holy Spirit will yield the Fruit of the Spirit." Here are the works of the flesh and their definitions so that you will know them and avoid them.

<u>Works of the flesh</u>

Adultery...............Being sexually unfaithful to your spouse
Fornication..............Sexual activities without being married
Uncleanness......A life that is not pure in moral or religious ways
Lasciviousness..............A lifestyle that says, "anything goes"
Idolatry.............When things in our life have priority over God
Witchcraft..........................Participation in drug activities
Hatred.............Strong negative feelings toward self or others
Variance.............….............To disagree, rival, dispute, or quarrel

Emulation....Dissension or rebellion against those in authority
Wrath...Malice, or ill will
Strife..Anger
Sedition..Selfishness
Heresy.................To go against accepted religious doctrine
Envying...Jealous rivalry
Murder...To kill
Drunkenness......................................Habitual drinking
Reveling......................Carousing, drunkenness, loudness

The Bible says people who do these things shall not inherit or share in the kingdom of God. As you grow stronger in the Lord you will develop a conscious will to avoid these activities in your life. Look now at what will happen when the Holy Spirit is abiding in your life and the fruit of the spirit is growing in you.

<u>Fruit of the Spirit</u>

Love - To share the grace of God with others in ways that help to strengthen the   spiritual and physical well being of others without looking for anything in return.
Joy - Inner happiness that depends on a personal relationship with Jesus, not events and things.
Peace - An inner calm assurance that comes from God.
Long- suffering – Patience rooted in hope
Gentleness - Tenderness
Faith - Complete trust in God
Goodness- Kindness
Meekness – Modesty can be humbled even with power or authority.
Temperance – The practice of self-control

As the fruit of the spirit grows in your life you will notice that the lust of the flesh will diminish. This is so because as a new creature in Christ your ways and attitudes that did not bring glory and honor to God will begin to go away.

Blessing #2 - Sin has no control over you.

In Romans the 6th Chapter the Apostle Paul offers three insights relating to sin and the believer.

Romans 6:1-11 - Sin has no power in your life - To put it plainly, you can't say "the devil made me do it," because he cannot. The Apostle Paul tells us that as protégé of Jesus we are dead to sin, meaning sin has no power in our lives. Paul explains in these verses that sin has no power over us because of our union with Jesus. Since sin cannot control Jesus it cannot control us. In other words our old sinful nature is subdued (in remission) we become a new person in Christ.

This point is important for you to know. As a protégé of Jesus there will be times when you will find yourself tempted to sin, and you will need to remember this thought: *"Because Jesus is my Savior, sin has as much power over me as death has over Jesus Christ, therefore the victory over sin is mine because Jesus has already conquered death."*

Now I want you to be clear on what I am telling you. Sin will never go away, and all of us will be tempted, but always remember that as children of God sin has no power or control in our lives.

Romans 6:12-22 - Don't let sin in your life - Since we now know that sin has no power in our life, we must put our knowledge into action by resisting sin in our life. If we choose to offend God by continuing to sin with our thoughts, words, and deeds, it is because we choose to do it.

God never forces His will in our lives. He wants us to accept him on our own. That is why he gives us the freedom to choose to accept or reject him. In verse 19 of Romans 6th chapter, Paul gives us a physical exercise to help us deal with sin and keep it from reigning in our lives.

Simply put, he tells us to take the energy that we used when we were in sin and use it to serve and glorify God. Use it to help someone, or to work in your church, or to study the interesting stories in the Bible. Use that energy to tell others about Jesus.

Romans 6:23 - Sin pays its debts eternally - Finally Paul makes one more observation about sin which also serves as a reason for being a victorious overcomer. Sin leads to destruction of the body, mind, and soul. It also leads to the destruction of the home, educational pursuits, marriages, ministries, finances and the list goes on. These are terrible prices to pay for sin. Sin separates us all from God. We cannot have true fellowship and continue to sin.

As you grow up in God, meet people and have many different experiences; remember, you are in charge of your actions, desires, and thoughts. **They are not in control of you.** You have the choice to please God or reject God's will. The choice is yours. True victory over sin belongs to **YOU** if you intend to serve the Lord using every tool and gift God makes available to you.

Have the attitude of the songwriter who wrote, "You know the road is rough and the going gets tough and the hills are hard to climb, but I started out a long time ago, there is no doubt in my mind, I've decided to make Jesus my choice." Remember sin has no power over you.

Blessing #3 - You will have the gift of the Holy Spirit.

When Jesus left his followers to return to his Father in heaven he told them to go to Jerusalem and wait until they received power. Acts chapter 2 tells us that when they were together, and on one accord, the Holy Spirit came as a rushing mighty wind filling them all with power. Make sure you read the second chapter of Acts for a complete understanding of what happened.

Jesus promised that the Holy Spirit would come to us as the spirit of truth, a comforter, a guide, and a teacher. Coming directly from God, the Holy Spirit would verify and support all that he had taught. Study the following scriptures.

♦ *"But theComforter, which is the Holy Ghost, whom the Father will send in my name, he shall teach you all things, and bring all things to your remembrance, whatsoever I have said unto you." John 14:26.*

♦ *"But when the Comforter is come, whom I will send unto you from the Father, even the Spirit of truth, which proceeded from the Father, he shall testify of me: And ye also shall bear witness, because ye have been with me from the beginning." John 15:26-27.*

♦ *"Nevertheless I tell you the truth; It is expedient for you that I go away: for if I go not away, the Comforter will not come unto you; but if I depart, I will send him unto you. And when he is come, he will reprove the world of sin, and of righteousness, and of judgment: Of sin, because they believe not on me; Of righteousness, because I go to my Father, and ye see me no more; Of judgment, because the prince of this world is judged. I have yet many things to say unto you, but ye cannot bear them now. Howbeit when he, the spirit of truth, is come, he will guide you into all truth: for he shall not speak of himself but whatsoever he shall hear, that shall he speak: and he will show you things to come. He shall glorify me: for he shall receive of mine, and shall show it unto you." John 16:7-14.*

As you grow in your understanding of the Holy Spirit you will notice that the Spirit is your companion. The Holy Spirit, from the time you receive Christ in your life, will lead and guide you in your growth and understanding as a child of God.

The Holy Spirit will also comfort and encourage you throughout your life as a Christian. This will be evidenced by the decline of the works of the flesh and the increase of the fruit of the spirit in your life. The Holy Spirit will also give you enabling power for effective service. Be it preaching, teaching, singing, evangelizing or anything else related to Christian service.

This enabling power can be understood as the anointing, which is a sign of God's approval of your service for Him, **Acts 10:37-38, Acts 3:6-10**. The Holy Spirit will also give you some specific gifts as recorded in **Romans 12:6-8, I Corinthians 12:4-11, Ephesians 4:11**.

When we started this chapter, I told you that Christ has a lot to offer you. In this chapter we looked at some benefits that come when we accept Jesus Christ's invitation to follow him and learn from him. Christ offers you an opportunity to achieve abundant life, complete with victory, success and the wisdom to accept and overcome life's most difficult experiences. Christ will also supply you with all the things that will help you achieve abundant life.

As you continue to read you will see how Jesus' invitation to abundant life as his protege' has both social and spiritual significance. As you read this book, read it with great hope and expectation because in this book there is a personal message from God just for you.

Quiz & Discussion

1) What is a protégé?
2) What does it mean to be a protégé of Jesus?
3) Name our spiritual enemies.
4) How can we overcome these enemies?
5) What were the four areas in which Jesus had it together?
6) How do you become a protégé of Jesus?
7) Name the three blessings that come when you become a protégé of Jesus.

Discussion: Are there any advantages to growing up as a protégé of Jesus? If so what are the advantages in contrast to a young person who is not a protégé of Jesus?

Chapter Two

"I can do all things through Christ who strengthens me." Philippians 4:13

Staring out as a protégé of Jesus, some of you will find yourselves tempted by the excitement of worldliness, the lust of the flesh, and the tricks of the devil. All of these things will hinder your growth and maturity as a protégé of Jesus if you let them.

Some of you may be tempted to go back to the habits and attitudes of your old sinful nature. Some of you will find it hard to let go of your past. Therefore, you must have the will and determination to overcome anything that will hinder your spiritual growth, maturity and fruitfulness.

Remember the blessings you received when you became a protégé of Jesus? You are a new creature in Christ, sin has no control over you and the Holy Spirit will strengthen and anoint you. But remember those blessings will not do you much good if you do not have the will and determination to overcome the hindrances you may encounter in life.

In this chapter we will look at some important things that will help you develop the will and determination to be victorious. To better understand the message of this chapter, look at the definitions of the words *worship* and *reverence*. These two action words are important in the process of being an overcoming protégé of Jesus.

Worship *- An expression of high adoration, reverence, trust, love, loyalty, and dependence on a higher power.*

Reverence *- A feeling or attitude of deep respect tinged with awe.*

In order to overcome the hindrances you will encounter in life, you must first have a reason to overcome something. Second, you must understand that the consequences of not striving to be an overcomer. Third, you must be committed to succeeding in whatever it is you are trying to overcome.

A Good Reason For Being An Overcomer

During the times that you feel discouraged and unable to overcome an obstacle, stumbling block, or pitfall, be encouraged by these words found in I John 4:4, which says, *"...Greater is He that is in you than He that is in the world."* In other words, the power of God is greater in you than the influences of the world, your flesh, and the trickery of the devil.

To help you overcome your uncontrolled thoughts, your lust, your bad habits, your prejudices or any other hindrances you will face as a protégé of Jesus you will need a good reason to overcome. In the story of Jesus praying in the garden of Gethsemane we read of a conflict that Jesus had. His conflict would have been a great hindrance to his success if he did not have a good reason for overcoming his conflict.

Jesus' conflict - In the 14th chapter of Mark, we are given the description of a spiritual struggle that Jesus went through while he was in the Garden of Gethsemane. The Bible tells us that Jesus went into the Garden of Gethsemane to pray.

As he prayed he said, *"Abba, Father, all things are possible unto thee; take away this cup from me: nevertheless not what I will, but what thou wilt," Mark 14:36.* The Bible tells us that Jesus prayed that prayer three times.

Imagine knowing that you are going to die an unjust death for the salvation of mankind and you asked your closest friends to pray with you for a while. Then you look at them after you have prayed and found them sleeping instead of praying with you. Wouldn't you feel terrible?

This is what happened to Jesus. His disciples, Peter, James, and John were his business associates. These were the men who he trusted and worked the closest with.

They enjoyed being on the Mount of Transfiguration with Jesus and experiencing the glory of God. They enjoyed being in the inner circle of Jesus and the prestige it brought, but when Jesus needed them to pray with him, they went to sleep. Now if it were you or me in Jesus' situation, we probably would have said, "forget it," but I am glad that Jesus said, "Nevertheless not my will but Thy will be done."

Each time I read this passage of scripture I am encouraged. I am encouraged because if Jesus could overcome his conflicts so can I. It is also encouraging to know that it was his love and faithful reverence to God that helped him to overcome his conflict. Jesus had to overcome his own self-will in order to do God's will. Some of the conflicts we all encounter that can become serious hindrances are:

- ♦ Having to forgive and love someone who has hurt you or someone you love.
- ♦ Having to use self-control when you want to physically hurt someone or give him or her a piece of you mind.
- ♦ The times you lose your self-control as it relates to sex, eating, the use of alcohol and drugs.
- ♦ When your body starts craving for satisfaction but you know satisfying your craving is unsatisfactory to God.

It is always easy to do the right thing when it does not cause a conflict with the inner self or between family and friends. But when Christian faith requires us to go beyond the limits of our attitude, discipline, and character to bring glory to God, it can cause a serious conflict within.

The crucible - In the Garden of Gethsemane Jesus was experiencing what I call a "crucible of fire." I call it a crucible of fire because a crucible is a vessel used to melt and test metals under extreme heat. When gold is tried in the fire, it is tried in a crucible that has been put into a furnace. After exposure to the heat it is melted and can then be molded.

Whenever we reach the point when it is hard to accept and follow the will of God, it may seem as if we have been placed into a crucible and then placed into a furnace where God molds us through our tests and trials. It is in the crucible experiences of life that we grow and become what God wants us to be. In Romans 5:3 Paul tells us, *"we glory in tribulation also because tribulation worketh patience, and patience experience, and experience hope."*

The difficult times in life make us stronger and help build our character. Jesus' crucible experience occurred in the Garden of Gethsemane. Moses' crucible experience occurred when God told him to go to Egypt and tell Pharaoh to free Israel. Elijah's crucible experience occurred in a cave while he was running from Jezebel and Jonah's crucible experience occurred in the belly of a large fish.

Many Christians struggling to overcome the hindrances in their life reach their crucible of fire when they realize that God wants a full commitment from them daily. The crucible for any of us can come because God requires us to love Him and our neighbors as ourselves not with an emotional love, but with the unselfish attitude of Agape love. Agape love is the act of unconditional brotherly love.

Many times we reach a point where we feel that we have given all that we can give of ourselves from our spiritual and physical substance. In fact, it seems impossible to go any further.

Mark 14:35 reveals the crucible experience of Jesus in the

33

garden of Gethsemane. Jesus was able to overcome his crucible of fire and say, *nevertheless not what I will, but what thou wilt,"* because of his reverence and love for God.

When we face the crucibles of fire in our lives that bring us to the edge of our faithful commitment to God, we must remember that we can find the will and motivation to be victorious overcomers through our reverence and love for God. To be a victorious overcomer we need to have working in us what Jesus had working in Him. When we do, we will have the strength and ability to do the things that seem impossible. Look at what Jesus had working for him in his life.

Jesus had a fellowship with God - Before we can make any kind of genuine commitment to God that will stand any test, we must have a fellowship with Jesus, a fellowship that is as real as any fellowship we have with our family or friends.

For our family or special friends, people will do much more than they will do for a stranger or casual acquaintance. For family or special friends we will tolerate more or put up with more than we would from a stranger or casual acquaintance.

Always remember that Jesus did not have a casual acquaintance with God nor was he a stranger to God. But he had an intimate relationship with God to the extent that when Jesus prayed he would call God His Father. Mark 14:36

Jesus told the disciples, *"If you have known me then you have known the Father." Jesus also said, "When you have seen me you have seen the Father," John 14:7.*

As a protégé of Jesus, what kind of fellowship do you want to have with Jesus everyday? Is it a casual fellowship? Is He an important part of your everyday life? As a protégé of Jesus, always make sure that your fellowship with Christ is a close fellowship.

Jesus was willing to do God's will - As a protégé of Jesus you must represent and glorify God with your life everyday. This involves knowing your purpose in life and fulfilling that purpose. In Matthew 5:13-16, Jesus teaches that as a believer, your purpose is to make a difference in the world by letting your light shine before the world.

Every talent, every skill, every spiritual gift and natural ability was given to you for a purpose. As a Christian that purpose is to represent Christ in your home, community, school, on your job, in your church, or wherever you may go. Jesus has called on all believers to be fishermen and ambassadors.

As a fisherman you can use your ability to lead others to Christ. By being an ambassador for Christ you can represent him by showing people how God is real in your life through your actions and deeds. Jesus said, "I must work the works of Him that sent me, while it is day: the night cometh, when no man can work." John 9:4 and *"Nevertheless not my will but Thy will be done," Mark 14:36,* because he knew his purpose in life.

As a protégé of Jesus your life has a definite purpose. When you know that you have a God-given purpose for living, you should be willing to say as does the hymn: "I'll bear the cross and endure the pain," because you know that God has given your life purpose.

The only way that you can really know what God's will is for your life is by having that personal fellowship with Him which consists of prayer, devotion and the study of His word.

Jesus wanted to glorify God - In the 17th chapter of John, Jesus prayed to God about his ministry and how his service was for the purpose of bringing Glory to God. As a protégé of Jesus you should know how to glorify the Lord. We can glorify the Lord by: *Praising Him, Psalms 22:23, Doing good works, Matthew 5:16, Being fruitful, John 15:8, Through spiritual* *unity, Romans 15:6, Being completely consecrated, I Corinthians 6:20.*

Jesus wanted to be an obedient, righteous, and faithful representative of God here on earth so when people saw him they would know that he was the Son of God. Jesus was able to say "nevertheless, not my will but thy will be done," because he wanted to glorify God with his total being.

It should be your desire to know the Lord intimately, to be obedient to the will of the Lord, and to glorify God in all you say and do. You can overcome the hindrances in your life when your reason for doing so is your love for the Lord and His love for you.

Avoiding The Consequences Of Failure

As you read the Bible, one fact keeps standing out. That fact is that God wants all Christians to live victorious lives. By victorious I mean that God wants us to live sanctified lives, free from sin's bondage. He wants us to be able to overcome the difficulties that may come in our lives with the confidence, authority and the dignity of Christ.

Another fact evident in the Bible is that God does not save us and fill us with the power of the Holy Ghost to fail. God has provided us with everything we need to live victorious lives. He has provided us with the Holy Ghost, His word, and a direct line to him through prayer. Then we have the added assurance that God cannot lie, therefore we can depend on his word. *Isaiah 55:11, II Timothy 1:12.*

Jesus was a victorious overcomer because he had a fellowship with God. The reason for failure among Christians to live victorious lives is that they don't realize that strength comes from daily fellowship through worship and service.

To best understand the importance of worship as strength in overcoming the temptations of the world, our human nature, and the trickery of the devil, consider the story of ancient Israel as recorded in Isaiah the 40th chapter.

The Cost - *"O Jacob, O Israel, how can you say that the Lord doesn't see your troubles and isn't being fair? Don't you understand? Don't you know by now that the everlasting God, the creator of the farthest parts of the earth, never grows faint, or weary? No one can fathom the depths of His understanding. He gives power to the tired and worn out, and strength to the weak. Even youth shall be exhausted, and young men will give up. But they that wait upon the Lord they shall renew their strength, they shall mount up with wings as eagles, they shall run and not get weary and they shall walk and not get faint." Isaiah 40:27-31, The Living Bible*

Israel, who was God's special people in the Old Testament, was once a powerful nation under the leadership of King Saul, King David and King Solomon. But by the time the prophet Isaiah wrote this passage of scripture Israel had been reduced to a weak troubled nation in exile because she forgot her reason and purpose for existing. God chose her to worship him and him only. Read the 20th Chapter of Exodus.

In return God made Israel a prosperous and strong nation. But Israel started backsliding as a nation. She was tempted by the influences of the world around her and she failed to faithfully honor and worship God. As a result, the nation of Israel became a prisoner of war.

Backsliding - *Going back into a sinful life.* Being a protégé of Jesus you must be careful not to backslide into sin and become Satan's SPOW (Spiritual Prisoners of War). Like Israel, we too can become weak and troubled prisoners of the spiritual warfare that Paul talks about in the sixth chapter of

Ephesians. We can lose the joy in our lives, in our homes and in our relationship with God and our fellow man, not because God has left us, but because we would have left God.

As young people facing the future and all of its uncertainties you need every advantage available to you so that you can be free from all forms of oppressive bondage that can hinder you in life. You need every advantage available to you so that you can be strong enough to overcome the temptations that would make you weak and vulnerable to failure.

I use Isaiah 40:27-31 to describe the cost of failure and how to avoid it because I once heard a preacher say an interesting thing about waiting on the Lord for your deliverance, power and victory. The preacher said that waiting on the Lord is like waiting on a customer in a restaurant. If you wait on a customer, giving him the best service that you can give and he thinks well of himself, he'll give you a good tip because he knows he is worthy of your service.

Avoiding Failure- The preacher continued to say that when we wait on God (render service to God) he will, through his Holy Ghost, give us power reminiscent of an eagle whose powerful wings can lift it above the storm. God gives us this enduring power so we won't get faint and we won't get weary.

To wait on the Lord does not mean sitting around doing nothing. It means to that we are doing something. When we wait on God we are actively involved in a relationship with Him. We are serving Him through worship, praise, helping others, and honoring Him. In return God blesses us with enabling power to overcome any and all the hindrances we may encounter in life. Jesus tells us in *John 15:5, "I am the vine, ye are the branches: He that abideth in me, and I in him, the same bringeth forth much fruit: for without me ye can do nothing."*

One of the things that make eating in a restaurant enjoyable is the quality of service. When the waiter or waitress waiting on your table demonstrates devotion, dedication, diligence, and the ability to follow directions, I enjoy giving them a larger tip. When their service is not good the tip won't be as large.

As a protégé of Jesus the time comes when the power of God seems weak in your life because you are having a hard time overcoming problems in your life. If you feel like you are spinning your wheels and are going nowhere, if you feel that God is distant from you and you feel that your prayers are not being answered, look at your quality of service to the Lord. The best way to avoid failure and be an overcomer is to serve the Lord with devotion, dedication, diligence, and obedience.

Practice Daily Devotions: If you are going to be strong in the Lord and in the power of His might then you must make sure that you take time to pray and read the Bible on a regular basis. Remember prayer and knowing God's Word will strengthen your fellowship with the Lord and keep the devil from successfully being able to lie to you. Read Psalms 119:105, I Thessalonians 5:17, John 8:31-32, Luke 22:40, Daniel 6:10.

Daily Dedication: Every day of your life you should reaffirm your commitment to God. You can do this by confessing your shortcomings and failures from the previous day and yielding yourself anew to the will of God for that day.

In my prayer time I've learned to say, *"Lord, I make myself available to you so your kingdom can come and your will may be done in my life and through my life today."* Everyday is a new day and we need new strength, and a renewed commitment. Read II Kings 23:3, Proverbs 23:26, Romans 12:1.

Daily Diligence: Everyday we must do some work in the Kingdom of God. You may have a gift for witnessing to others about Jesus. Your gift might be in intercessory prayer, which means praying for others. You might be good with helping the elderly. You might be good at explaining the scriptures to family and friends. Whatever you can do to encourage others in Christ, do it. Read Hebrews 3:13, Matthew 5:16.

Direction: Victory comes when we follow the lead of the Holy Spirit. The Holy Spirit as a companion will guide and direct you everyday in the will of God. Each of us has to learn how to be still and quiet enough to hear what the Spirit says to us.

There will be those times in your life when the Spirit will tell you to be patient. You may not want to be patient but you will always do better to follow the prompting of the Holy Spirit. You may not want to forgive someone for doing you wrong, but when the spirit speaks to you and says forgive, you will do well to forgive.

Someone might say, "How will I know if and when the Holy Spirit is speaking to me?" You will always know the prompting of the Spirit because it will always seek to do two things with you. It will always lead you in truth, and it will always seek to bring glory and honor to God.

In the evening session during one of our summer break youth conferences; we heard the testimony of a former drug addict who is now clean, saved, filled with the Holy Spirit, and he is a pastor with a great anointing. That night I was scheduled to bring the message after his testimonial.

The man's testimony was very powerful and the presence of God was in the auditorium. The Holy Spirit said to me as he finished with his testimony, "Have him offer an invitation." I was obedient to the Holy Spirit.

I know now that God was testing me to see if I would be obedient to His direction. Because of my obedience, God got the glory and all of us got a lesson in yielding to the Holy Spirit. Learn how to listen to God so that you can hear his voice and obey.

Victory Requires Commitment

Finally, if you are going to overcome all things through Christ Jesus you cannot quit every time the going gets rough or things do not go your way. This is true in every area of your life. Jesus was never a quitter. He knew his mission in life and stayed focused on his goal regardless of the obstacles he encountered. Our society has too many quitters and we don't need anymore. Don't be a quitter.

One of the most passionate proclamations of commitment found in the Bible is found in Romans the 8th chapter. The Apostle Paul was a man who had good reason to quit but was committed not to do so. Listen to his testimony.

"Who shall separate us from the love of Christ? Shall tribulation, or distress, or persecution, or famine, or nakedness, or peril, or sword? As it is written: For thy sake we are killed all day long; we are accounted as sheep for the slaughter. Nay, in all things we are more than conquerors through him that loved us.

For I am persuaded, that neither death, nor life, nor angels, nor principalities, nor powers, nor things present, nor things to come, nor height, nor depth, nor any other creature, shall be able to separate us from the love God, which is in Christ Jesus our Lord." Romans 8:35-39.

Paul's personal commitment is so strong that he states that nothing will cause not only him, but also the whole church to be separated from God's love. Then he lists a number of life's situations that can be conquered through Christ who gives us strength.

His testimony has significance in all of our lives because there is a lack of commitment among people, young and old alike, when it comes to coping with the difficult and stressful times in our lives and when it comes to maintaining personal discipline.

Life can sometimes be difficult and painful, but if you intend to succeed as a Christian and achieve abundant life, you must have a strong commitment to be steadfast in the Faith and in your endeavors in life. Excuses for giving up can be many, and to you, they may really be valid. However, you should always remember that excuses have hindered or destroyed the potential success of many people. Don't let excuses stop you from achieving victory and productivity in your life.

The Apostle Paul had good reason to quit, but he chose to stay the course. Here is a man who encountered problems constantly throughout his ministry. In fact, the greater the success experienced by Paul in his ministry, the more tribulations he went through.

In Acts 19:23-41 you can read about how a town turned against him because he was effective in leading people to Christ. In II Corinthians 12:7 you can read his testimony of how his body was under the attack of Satan's messenger.

In Acts 16:16-18 you can also read about an evil spirit that disrupted his evangelistic crusade. All this and much more occurred in Paul's ministry because it was Jesus' will for Paul to suffer much for Christ's sake as a servant of the Lord, Act 9:16.

In spite of the obstacles and difficulties, Paul was determined to press forward with commitment, and he did. At the end of his life he was able to look back and say to his protégé, Timothy, *"For I am now ready to be offered, and the time of my departure is at hand. I have fought a good fight, I have finished my course, I have kept the faith."* II Timothy 4:6-7

As a protégé of Jesus, be committed to overcoming obstacles that will keep you from being all that God wants you to be and having all that God wants you to have. Be committed to knowing God's will for your life and be obedient to that will. Every time you are confronted with obstacles that make you want to give up, just remember these words: *"I can do all things through Christ who strengthens me," Philippians 4:13*

You can make it if you have the will to succeed. As a protégé of Jesus you have a good reason to succeed. You know what it takes to succeed, you know the result of failure, and you now know how important commitment is.

YOU CAN MAKE IT!!!

Quiz & Discussion

1) What are the three things needed in order to be an over-comer?
2) What was Jesus' conflict?
3) Name three reasons why Jesus overcame his conflict.
4) What four things does God provide us to help us avoid failure?
5) What does it mean to wait on God?
6) Name four things that we can do to avoid failure as an overcomer.
7) Being committed to overcoming and serving God mean you will not be a _____.

Discussion:
1. Why is it important to have a will and determination to be an overcomer?
2. What are some things that Christian teenagers need to overcome?

Chapter Three

"Be not deceived. God is not mocked. Whatsoever a man shall sow, that which he sows he shall reap. He that soweth to the flesh shall of the flesh reap corruption. He that soweth to the spirit shall of the spirit reap life everlasting," *Galatians 6:7.*

In this chapter we will look at four common sense principles based on God's Word. These principles will help you to mature and prosper in both your physical and spiritual life.

What Goes Around Comes Around

The first principle is "what goes around, comes around." Your success in life depends on what you contribute to life and how you treat people. By allowing the Holy Spirit to dwell in you and guide you in fulfilling God's purpose for your life, you will experience abundant life. Likewise, if all your efforts in life are mainly based on selfish desires without regard for God and others, you will experience a life of emptiness and loneliness.

As a protégé of Jesus you do not have to be mean, dirty, and cutthroat to succeed in life. You do not have to be jealous of someone else's talent or ability, nor do you have any reason to feel threatened or intimidated by others. All you have to do is treat people with the respect and dignity that you want to be treated with.

Jesus made this point clear when he said, *"Therefore all things whatsoever ye would do that men should do to you, do ye even so to them; for this is the law and the prophets."* *Matthew 7:12.*

44

Micah the 6th chapter says, *"What doth the Lord require? He hath showed thee, O man, what is good; and what doth the Lord require of thee, but to do justly, and to love mercy, and to walk humbly with thy God,"* Micah 6:8.

Look with me at the stories of King Saul and Joseph the Dreamer. Both of these men were called at a young age to lead and protect God's people. It is interesting to note that when Saul started his service for God as King over Israel, he had a great deal of prestige and people looked up to Saul with honor, respect, hope and anticipation. Joseph, on the other hand, started his service for God as the most unlikely person to succeed. His brothers did not think much of him, so they sold him into slavery hoping that he would be lost and forgotten.

Saul sowed seeds of disobedience that involved selfishness, jealousy, hatred, and strife. This led to his decline and fall. But Joseph sowed seeds of love, peace, honesty, faithfulness, and patience, which led him to great success. The story of these two men remind us that opportunity can knock at our door, but if our attitude and disposition is not right we will inevitably fail.

Saul & David's Story - I Samuel

Saul reaped destruction in his life because as God's chosen vessel he was selfish and disobedient to God's will. Read Chapters 13 and 15 of 1 Samuel. When Saul realized that his world was coming apart and David, the shepherd boy, was growing in respect and notoriety among the Israelis, Saul began to react negatively to David. He reacted with strife, hatred, intimidation, jealousy, and he even attempted to murder David.

Saul sowed seeds of the flesh and he got in return separation from God, inner turmoil, and death. Most people would have responded with bitterness to Saul for the bad things he did, but David did not. In spite of all that Saul was doing to him, David loved Saul, respected him, and defended him.

David had two opportunities to kill King Saul when he caught him at a disadvantage. His advisors told him to end his problems with Saul and kill him. But David did not because he knew Saul was the anointed of the Lord. Read the 24th and 26th Chapters of I Samuel.

David, for the most part, was not selfish in his dealings with people. When David did make mistakes he confessed his sins to God, and asked for forgiveness. A protégé of Jesus must not become so full of pride that he or she cannot say "I'm sorry" to God or other people especially when they are wrong or have hurt someone.

Pride - Implies an exalted opinion of oneself often bolstered by a lower opinion of others. The Bible states, *"Pride goeth before destruction, and a haughty spirit before a fall," Proverbs 16:18.*

David's reward for his faithfulness and humility was God's anointing and the throne of Israel. Here are some other scriptures that you can read about the danger of pride. Psalms 10:2, 73:6, Proverbs 11:2, 21:4, 28:25, I John 2:16.

Joseph and His Brothers - Genesis 37-45

Joseph's situation was different in that from a seventeen-year old boy until the age of thirty, Joseph was first a slave and then a prisoner because of the evil deeds of others. His experience as a slave began when his jealous brothers sold him into slavery leading their father to believe Joseph was dead.

God blessed Joseph in such a way that everything Joseph did, he did well. As a slave God blessed Joseph with the gift of administration and he ran the business affairs of Potiphar, the chief guard of Pharaoh's army. All was well with Joseph until Potiphar's wife accused him of rape and he was thrown into prison.

When in prison, Joseph was given charge over the prisoners in the jailhouse. Joseph's opportunity for freedom came when Pharaoh called on him to interpret a dream many years after Joseph was put into prison. When Joseph interpreted the dream of Pharaoh, Pharaoh was pleased with Joseph and made him Governor of Egypt. As Governor, Joseph was in charge of the department of agriculture.

When Joseph's family became victims of a great famine, Jacob, Joseph's father sent his sons to Egypt to buy food. Unaware of God's blessing, they had no idea that their long lost brother Joseph was the Governor of Egypt.

One of the lessons to be learned from the story of Joseph is that throughout our lives we should always be careful how we treat people because we do not know what the future holds, whom we will need and who will need us.

As soon as Joseph saw his brothers coming to buy food, he knew who they were. Instead of being vindictive or spiteful to his brothers for their injustice, Joseph knew that God's purpose for his life was being fulfilled. Joseph knew that all he had gone through put him in a position to save his family from certain death. Joseph eventually explained who he was to his brothers and forgave them for their wrong doings.

Always be careful to treat people right. My mother taught me a valuable lesson when she said, "Always be careful how you treat people in life. Most likely the same people you step on and mistreat going up the ladder of success, you will meet coming back down that same ladder."

Your Value of Hard Work Is Important

The second principle that you should always remember is that nothing worth having will come easy. You have to work at achieving the things in life you want and this involves developing a serious work ethic. If you don't work, you won't be able to take care of yourself and your responsibilities. No work, no pay.

This work ethic must apply in your studies, in your prayer and Bible study time, in the quality of work you do on the job, and in the quality of relationships you have with people. This work ethic must also apply as you care for your mind, body, and spirit.

Many young people believe that the best things in life come free and easy. When it comes to doing schoolwork, a number of young people will not do their schoolwork. And if they do, they do not want to do their best. Some young people, maybe even you, believe that your parents and the world owe you a free ride. But that is just not true.

Hard work ought to be a welcome part of every teenager and young adult's life. I say this because hard work will help to mold your character. Hard work will also help you to appreciate the things that you have, and it will also give people a reason to respect you.

Some of you might say, "Well jobs are hard to get." That may be true. Economy opportunities for African American males are not the best. But that is no excuse to give up and look for an easy way to make it in life. Anyone who tries to make quick and easy money, especially outside of the law, is headed down a path of destruction.

Most of you have natural talents and abilities. That natural talent and ability will bring you income if you learn how to package and market it as a service that will meet a need for others. If you think you don't have a natural ability, you certainly can learn how to do something productive on your own if you really want to benefit financially.

Many people do not see college as an alternative for them. Some people don't see the military as a way to get a start in life and the reality is that very, very few young men are going to make it into professional sports. Too many young men think that they are going to make it in professional sports. It is not impossible, but it is not likely. The safe thing to do as you hold on to your dream to be in professional sports is to prepare yourself to do something else.

In one of our youth conferences a brother by the name of Richard E. Blackmore, a former football player for the Philadelphia Eagles and the San Francisco Giants, spoke. He explained to the audience that being an ex-football player did not carry a lot of weight in the everyday job market.

He pointed out that it did not matter that he was a part of a Super Bowl team with a Super Bowl ring. It did not matter that he played with Joe Montana, Jerry Rice, or Randal Cunningham. What mattered was that he had prepared for life after football. Mr. Blackmore now runs his own successful computer systems business in Jackson, Mississippi.

My friend, Dexter Criss pretty much taught himself how to play the piano. After years of practice, he has developed into a good church musician. I have another friend, Terence Harris, author of "The Negro Creed and the Nurses Creed," who told me how someone could make money by cleaning aquariums for people who do not have the time or patience to clean their own.

There are many people who mow lawns in the summer and shovel snow in the winter to make money. Even though jobs are hard to get, if you can learn how to offer quality services to your community, your church, or your organization, you can make it. It will also help you tremendously if you work with other ambitious people through networking. If you persevere, you can make it. If you can't find a job, use your imagination to start a small business and make it work.

When I was sixteen years old I offered personalized car care services to the members of my church. I washed, hand waxed, and buffed their cars. I had three prices: one for compact cars, one for mid-size cars and one for large cars. I would schedule my clients and then meet them on time to do the job. I made it a point to do an exceptional job so my clients would let me do it again, and tell others about my service. As I grew up, God blessed me on many occasions to work and make money in a legal way.

There are a number of books and short stories written about men and women who rose from the difficulties of their day to make themselves successful in this life. Go to the library and look for those stories and be encouraged to work hard and make something of yourself.

The "Godfather of Soul," James Brown sang a song that said, "I don't want nobody to give me nothing, open up the door, I'll get it myself." That is a good attitude to have in this day and time. But always remember that many times the only doors that will open for you are the ones you open for yourself, by the grace of God.

Nothing in life comes free and you have to work hard to keep and maintain whatever you have or have accomplished in life. Look at the following scriptures that speak on the importance of a good work ethic.

"He becometh poor that dealeth with a slack hand: but the hand of the diligent maketh rich. He that gathereth in

summer is a wise son: but he that sleepeth in harvest is a son that causeth shame," Proverbs 10:4-5.

"The soul of the sluggard desireth, and hath nothing: but the soul of the diligent shall be made fat," Proverbs 13:4.

"He that tilleth his land shall be satisfied with bread: but he that followeth vain persons is void of understanding," Proverbs 12:11.

"Wealth gotten by vanity shall be diminished: but he that gathereth by labor shall increase," Proverbs 13:11.

"Not slothful in business; fervent in spirit; serving the Lord" Romans 12:11.

You Are Too Legit to Quit

The third principle that you should be aware is that you are too legit to quit. In other words you are too valuable to God and mankind to give up on reaching your full potential and fulfilling your God-given purpose in life. You are too legit to quit because you are a part of God's creation and everything that God created is good, Genesis 1:31.

Because you can sow in the spirit and reap the harvest of an abundant life as a protégé of Jesus, you are too legit to quit! Therefore, you should not allow the prejudices of others, difficult times, or the lack of other people's faith in you to stop you. You must learn how to press forward to achieve your purpose and goal in life.

If you make mistakes and experience failure, do not give up. All mistakes and failures can be made into stepping stones to success. Because you are too legit to quit, you must not give up on life when the chips are down, but instead use your God-given abilities and be fruitful. Remember that failure is success turned inside out!

Since you are too legit to quit, you can use the tools that God has given you to make your ideas and dreams a reality.

In the 25th chapter of Matthew there is a parable about a man who was about to leave the country. Before he left, he gave three of his servant's talents. The first servant he gave five talents, the second servant he gave two talents, the third servant he gave one talent.

The Bible tells us that he gave these talents according to their ability. When the man returned from his trip the first two servants used their talents but the third servant did not. As a result, the third servant lost what he had and was labeled by the man as *"the unprofitable servant."*

There are two possible reasons why the third servant became the unprofitable servant. First, it is possible that he was afraid to use what he had, not because it was so little, but because he doubted his own ability to achieve. Second, it is possible that he was too busy playing around and not taking his responsibility seriously.

My sister is a prominent lawyer in Pittsburgh, Pennsylvania. She shared with me the fact that many young people are unprofitable to society because they lack the basic skills and abilities necessary for gaining employment, such as thinking and being able to analyze. Hopefully, each of you will apply yourself to a personal quest of learning, achieving, and exercising the courage to use whatever gift, talent or ability you have to make your mark in the world. By doing so no one will be justified in calling you an unprofitable participant in society.

Consider living with this attitude: *"I would rather step out on faith and do my best to fulfill the purpose God has for my life by using all that God has given me. I will not live my life without trying to fulfill His purpose for my life because of doubt, fear and irresponsibility. When I get old I will be satisfied and fulfilled knowing that I did my best to achieve God's purpose and goals for my life."*

The Tools God Gives Each of Us

Did you know that God empowers us with the tools that will make us successful in life? In the book, "Think and Grow Rich, A Black Choice," the authors, Dennis Kimbro and Nepolian Hill, outline a list of things that enable people to successfully establish and achieve goals, face the challenges in their lives, and make an impact on the world. I see these things as working tools from God.

Imagination: God has given us the tool of imagination for the purpose of visualizing in our mind our ideas and thoughts. Imagination is the drafting board of our minds where we create the blue prints that make our ideas take shape so they can become a reality.

Desire: God has given us the tool of desire as a motivating force. Desire motivates us to turn our ideas and thoughts into reality. The greater your desire the harder you will work to make it happen.

Faith: The tool of faith is your personal confidence that your goal can and will become a reality. This is an important tool because sometimes people won't see or agree with your vision. They may criticize it, doubt it, and try to discourage you.

You should spend time with other people who have a positive faith like yours. You need to be around people who have stepped out on faith to achieve their goal. A good example of faith is found in the 13th chapter of Numbers when Moses sent twelve spies to scope out the land that God told Israel they could conquer and have.

When the spies brought their report back to Moses, ten spies said they could not conquer the land. But the other two spies, Joshua and Caleb, said that they could. Remember that

God had already told Israel they could possess the land. Because of the spies' report, Israel had to wait forty years before they were able to move into the Promise Land that God already said they could have forty years before.

All of the ten spies who said that they could not conquer the land died along with their families, in the wilderness. Jacob and Caleb were the only two original spies who lived through the wilderness experience and made it into the Promise Land. Take this thought with you through life, "You have to have faith to make your goals a reality."

Self-esteem: As a tool, self-esteem is an indication of your self-worth. Self-esteem is defined as "having a respectful and favorable impression of oneself. "If you don't think well of yourself, or what you are trying to do then do not expect people to think well of you or your hopes and dreams.

Self-reliance: Self-reliance means relying on your own power and ability to get the job done. If you wait on someone else to do for you what you should do for yourself; you will never achieve real success. God enables us, people will help us, but it is up to self to get the job done. No one can make you do well in school. No one can make you achieve. Only you can make yourself do these things.

Perseverance: Perseverance means being committed to seeing the goal met or the job done. When things go bad or mistakes have been made, that's when you must use this tool from God. Jesus said in Matthew 24:13, *"He that endureth to the end the same shall be saved."*

Enthusiasm: Enthusiasm is an essential tool because without enthusiasm you cannot motivate the interest of others in your goals and ideas. As a minister of the gospel, I am enthusiastic about the gospel of Jesus. My enthusiasm is evident in my preaching, teaching, singing, and writing. Teachers must be enthusiastic about what they are teaching, and doctors have to be enthusiastic about healing. I hope you get the picture because enthusiasm is an essential tool for success.

A Positive Personality: This is an important tool. If people don't like you, it doesn't matter how good, gifted, and smart you are, you will turn them off before they can experience your gifts, skills, and talent. We have to keep developing our personality and learn people-skills that will enhance whatever gifts, talents, or abilities we have.

As you become more familiar with these tools and how they can and do work in your life you will be able to live a fruitful life. In the book, "Think and Grow Rich, A Black Choice," by Dennis Kimbro and Nepolian Hill, seven components of a wealthy life are identified. These seven components are a good representation of a fruitful life for a protégé of Jesus for three reasons . . . 1. The significance of these components goes beyond money and material. 2. Each of these components involves the giving of oneself and the rewards that come in return. 3. This description of a fruitful life is also meaningful because the Word of God supports each component.

The Components of A Fruitful Life

Peace of Mind: Peace of mind is the inner calm that you have because you completely trust God. Peace of mind grows from your daily fellowship with Jesus and the presence of the Holy Spirit in your life. With peace of mind you have the confidence that all things will work out all right because God is in control. John 14:27, 16:33.

A Good Mental Attitude: My grandfather instilled this thought into the minds of his children and my mother instilled it in me. It is an important aspect in abundant living so I share it with you. "Accentuate the positives, eliminate the negatives, and don't mess around in between." Matthew 5:43-48, 6:19-34, Philippians 4.

Good Health: Our mind and our bodies are the vessels that God uses to contain our life force so we can live on this earth. We must take care of them; they are important aspects of abundant living. Mark 1: 26, Matthew 17:14-18, Luke 14:2-4, I Corinthians 6:19,20.

The Love and Respect of Others: The only people in the world who love you may be your family, but we must live in such a way that people will respect us even if they don't like us. John 15:12, Matthew 7:12, Luke 6:31

The Ability to Make a Living through a Strong Work Ethic: This aspect of abundant life allows you to live life standing on your own two feet. You can have the things you need and want while still helping others. Luke 5:1-7, II Thessalonians 3:8

Knowing Your Purpose in Life: One of the greatest blessings in life is to have and know that you have a specific purpose in life in serving God, Christ and mankind. Luke 10:30-36, John 9:4, Mark 1:16-20.

Fulfilling Your Purpose in Life: The opportunity to use our abilities to fulfill our purpose in life adds a tremendous sense of worth and meaning. Mathew 11:1-6

As a protege of Jesus, being guided by the indwelling of the Holy Spirit and using the tools that God has given you, the investment of your life in Jesus Christ will yield a life of fruitfulness, success, and prosperity.

Don't Be the Devil's Fool

As you find yourself experiencing the blessings that come from being a protégé of Jesus do not ever forget that it is God who is doing the blessing. Don't ever get the big head or forget where the Lord has brought you. The fourth principle is don't let the devil play you for a chump by stealing your victory.

In the third chapter of Genesis we will find the classic story of how the devil worked on Eve and made a fool out of her in the Garden of Eden, convincing her to eat from the Tree of Knowledge.

After reading that story in the Bible, it was easy for me to see how the devil has been making fools out of so many of our young people across America robbing and destroying their lives, hopes, and dreams.

The devil has a way of lying to your mind and deceiving you to the point that you are not sure of what is right and what is wrong. That's why Paul wrote in I Timothy 2:4 that it is God's will for all to be saved and know the truth.

As a protégé of Jesus you have to know where to draw the line when it comes to sowing seeds that please God and sowing seeds that will hurt you. I have been asked if dancing is bad, if rap music is bad, and so on. In response, I'll say "all rap music isn't bad, all movies are not bad, all television programs are not bad, all of our friends are not bad, all the places that we go are not bad. But if you do not know how to distinguish what is spiritually, mentally and physically healthy for you from what is not, you may very well end up like Eve losing all that God has given you."

Anything that will separate you from the love and fellowship of God is bad for you. Anything that is just as or more important to you than your fellowship with Jesus Christ is bad for you. The forbidden fruit for Eve was fruit from the tree of knowledge. Today the forbidden fruit for any Christian is anything that will harm your mind, body, and spirit.

Look closely with me at verses 1-6 in the third chapter of

Genesis. Notice how Satan deceived Eve. He will deceive us the same way if we let him. Eve was in the security of the garden with everything she needed available to her.

The only requirement she had to honor was to leave the fruit alone that was on the Tree of Knowledge because the penalty for eating from it would be death. But the devil convinced Eve that it was all right to eat from that tree.

You may come from a loving family with the security of a good home. Others of you may not have the ideal family or home life but you feel secure in your tremendous talent and ability. Whatever your condition in life may be, the devil will lie to you every time you put your guard down. When you put your guard down you give the devil an opportunity to plant a seed of destruction within you. The same way the devil lied to Eve, he will lie to you.

The same way the devil lied to Jesus during his temptation in the wilderness, he will lie to you. Read Mark Chapter 4. The devil does it by planting seeds of deception and destruction in our minds, and every time we lie to ourselves and receive those seeds of destruction, we become the devil's fool.

About Sex

One of the biggest ways the devil deceives Christians is through the misunderstanding about sex. The devil would like you to believe that sex before marriage and outside of marriage is good, healthy and wise. But the devil is a liar and does not let you know the downside of premarital sex until it is too late. Just as he tempted Eve to eat from the Tree of Knowledge he will tempt you to indulge in sex before marriage. Here's what I mean.

As a teenager's body grows and matures, so does the sexual feeling and desire. This is a part of the natural order of

God's creation. It is perfectly normal that you are developing a normal, healthy sexual drive to be used to fulfill one of the expressions of love after you get married.

As a protégé of Jesus you should understand that sexual desires and feelings become unhealthy when you allow them to control your mind and emotions. You must not let your mind and emotions control your sexual desires and feelings. It is also unhealthy when you view sexual feelings and desires as a green light to participate in premarital sex.

It is unfortunate, but your sexual desires are greatly stimulated by the influences around you. Your desire to participate in sex is influenced by your friends, television, advertisements, radio, videos, and movies. All of these things influence your mind with sexual images. Everyday of your life and almost everywhere you go you are bombarded with sex.

Sex has become so free and open in America that many children do not know that they should say no to sex, the same way they should say no to drugs. Since the AIDS epidemic, people have been speaking out and saying that since it is impractical to say no to sex, just practice safe sex.

In the past, some churches and schools issued condoms to prevent the spread of AIDS among those who refused to stop having sex. This may be good in principle and may very well help, but as a protégé of Jesus you should not participate in sexual activities until after marriage. I know that this may be hard for some of you, but remember what you read in the last chapter? You have a good reason to say no to sex, because you know the consequences of sin.

Many young people who have participated in sex, hoping to find love, comfort, and emotional or financial support have ended up suffering emotional and physical pain: emotional pain in the form of depression, guilt, mental anguish, anger, and problems with your family. Physically your life becomes vulnerable to venereal diseases and unwanted pregnancies.

My suggestion to you is to resist sex until you get married. This is the will of God. I know that many of you are saying "that's easier said than done," so I want you to consider this point of view to be in line with God's will and hopefully you will be able to overcome it.

I recall a high school student telling me that I sounded like her father. Many of you may have heard this before, but if this is something that is hard for you to accept or deal with, just remember, you shall know the truth, and **"The Truth Shall Set You Free!"**

Another View

There is nothing difficult about jumping in and out of bed for a sexual thrill. But it is a great accomplishment to preserve your love with someone who is worthy of your love, trust, and commitment through marriage, which will be honored by God and your family.

The physical experience of making love through sexual intercourse is the ultimate physical gift from God to be shared between a husband and wife. But if you open and use the gift before marriage, it is like using a credit card so much that when you get paid, you can't enjoy your money because you used it up in credit with the added expenses of finance charges and interest.

Opening and using God's gift that was intended for a husband and wife before it is time is also like chipping a precious stone while trying to create a sculpture, then realizing that you chipped so much away that it can never be replaced. Don't be so quick to find a sex partner or lover.

Getting to the point in life where you can find the right

partner for marriage involves the following and more:

1. It involves finding someone who is compatible with you.
2. Someone who you can share mutual understanding with.
3. It means finding someone who along with you is willing to be committed to you for a lifetime.

This is a tedious and sometimes difficult point to reach. But if you view sex, relationships, and marriage as you would any other important aspect of your life that requires you to work, grow, plan, and be patient to achieve your goal, you will not go wrong. A pure, fulfilling, honorable sexual relationship inside the boundaries of wedlock should be as important as experiencing abundant life, getting a good education, finding a well - paying job or any other important goal in your life that requires hard work and discipline.

Another high school student once asked me, "Well suppose I do as you suggest and after I get married, my husband does not like having sex with me?" If you are going to marry because of sex then you are going to have a problem because it is difficult to build a lifetime relationship on sex alone.

Real love in a marriage involves friendship, romance (which is not the same as sex), a bond, and an unconditional love that expects nothing in return (Agape). Love that involves sex without some, if not all, of the others aspects of love, leaves a lot to be desired. All of these things contribute to a lasting and powerful love between husband and wife.

As a protégé of Jesus don't let the devil play you for a chump by leading you to believing that fornication is all right. Look at what God's word says about sex:

"Flee fornication. Every sin that a man does is without the body; but he that committeth fornication sinneth against

his own body." I Corinthians 6:18

"Nevertheless, to avoid fornication let every man have his own wife, and let every woman have her own husband." I Corinthians 7:2

No doubt about it, sex before marriage is a forbidden fruit.

The Devil is Busy

The devil will try to make a fool out of you in other ways too if you are not careful. He lies to many young people making them think that it is all right to participate in gang-violence and drug abuse. He will lead you to believe that it is all right to be disrespectful to your parents and other adults. The devil will lead you to believe that education is not important. The truth is that the evil one will confuse your mind and your thought processes.

Another way in which the devil has done great harm is by getting young men and women to forget, or overlook their heritage and the blood, sweat, and tears of their forefathers who have labored in this country either as slaves or free men. I believe this has a lot to do with the insensitivity that many young people have towards the value of life.

I am reminded of a story that an evangelist told about a young man who left his gang after receiving Christ in his life. The young man received Christ as his Savior and Lord at a youth revival. He was filled with the Holy Spirit and speaking in other tongues. But he allowed the devil to make a fool out of him. After being delivered from the hands of the enemy, this young man went back into the old neighborhood, ended up doing the same old things, and got into trouble.

One night the police were summoned to the scene where the young man had a gun in his hand. For fear of his life a police officer emptied his gun into the young man's body. The evangelist said that when he accompanied the young man's mother to the morgue, the policeman who shot the boy pulled the evangelist aside and told him:

"We had to do it. We knew all along that he was no good, we just had to do it. When we opened up his shirt, we knew that he would not make it waiting for an ambulance; we put him into the back seat of the squad car and rushed him to the hospital but he was dead by the time we got him there.

But Preacher, on the way to the hospital, a strange thing happened. He started crying out Jesus, I'm sorry, Jesus I'm sorry and then all of a sudden he started speaking in some unknown tongue that we couldn't understand." The evangelist concluded the story by saying that he believed that the young fellow repented and went home to be with Jesus.

One of the greatest joys of having salvation is that God will forgive us of our sins. If you made mistakes that are unacceptable to God, if you have hurt people, if you have gotten away from your purpose in life, I want you to be encouraged and know that God will forgive you.

When God forgives you do not allow the devil or anyone to make you feel guilty. The scriptures say, *"If we confess our sin, He is faithful and just to forgive us our sins, and cleanse us from all unrighteousness,"* I John 1:9.

God forgives sins but remember that when we choose to sin we still have to suffer the consequences. There are no guarantees that you will be as fortunate to seek forgiveness in the midst of death as did the young man who backslid into sin. So don't take that chance. Do not jeopardize your fellowship with Jesus.

The Devil is A Loser

When you find yourself being tempted by the devil just remember that he is a loser. He lost in heaven when the arch angel Michael whipped him and cast him out of heaven. Revelation 12:17-12.

The devil lost in Joseph's tomb when Jesus defeated death and rose from the dead with all power in heaven and in earth. The devil is the fool and he knows he's going to lose in the battle of Armageddon.

I believe that is why he is working so hard to destroy the minds, bodies, and souls of so many young people. The youth of today are the leaders of the new millennium. If the devil can keep young people confused and messed up today, he can have more control over humanity in the future. But he also knows that you have power over him (James 4:7) and he doesn't want you to know that.

Just as he lied to Eve, he will lie to keep you in darkness so that you will lose your blessing. But the victory is yours. You can keep the devil under your feet! My brothers and sisters, experience abundant life and don't let the devil rip you off.

In order for God to bless you with the best things in life, you have to give your best to life. You can do this by treating people like you want them to treat you. Don't be afraid of honest, hard work because it builds character. Don't give up when things don't go your way. Be persistent in your endeavors, glorify God in your efforts and the victory will be yours. Remember, you will reap what you sow.

Quiz & Discussion

1. Name the four principles in chapter three that will help you mature and prosper in both your physical and spiritual life.
2. What happens when you allow the Holy Spirit to dwell in you and guide you in fulfilling God's purpose for your life?
3. What happens when all your efforts in life are mainly based on selfish desires without regard for God and others?
4. What is one of the lessons to be learned from the story of Joseph?
5. Name the God-given tools that enable people to establish and achieve their goals, face the challenges in their lives, and make an impact on the world.
6. Name the seven components of a fruitful life.
7. What is a possible reason for the devil's attempt to destroy the mind, body, and soul of young people?

Discussion:
1. Is sex really the forbidden fruit before marriage? If so, Why?
2. Explain some ways protégés of Jesus should cope with the issue of sexual desire.

Chapter Four

"Trust in the Lord with all thine heart and lean not to thy own understanding. But in all thy ways acknowledge Him and he shall direct thy path, " Proverbs 3:5-6.

In this chapter we will talk about human frailty, look at the three things that cause pain and suffering and four ways to demonstrate your trust in God.

Man Is In Control But Not In Charge

One of the truths that we all must face is that there are many things in life that are out of our control. Humanity ultimately has no control over the powers of God. God allows us to know some of the mysteries of life and death, but man will only know or control as much as God allows.

For example, when it comes to the awesome powers of nature, God has allowed mankind to understand what causes earthquakes, tidal waves, hurricanes, tornadoes, and volcanic eruptions. Yet man cannot stop or control these forces.

God has allowed mankind to create all kinds of medicines from technology and research to find cures and help heal those who are sick and afflicted. Yet, we still do not have a cure for the common cold. We have made strides in a cure for cancer, but we still have not found a complete cure. We have made progress in AIDS research, but we still have no cure.

Progress in medicine can very often postpone our date with death for a little while but eventually we will answer death's call. When you consider how fragile human life is, it makes me wonder how humans can be so arrogant, insensitive to each other, God, and our environment.

Three Causes of Pain and Suffering

Our Personal Actions

Often in life we experience suffering or face situations that are out of our control because of things we have said and done. Whenever we make a decision, be it good or bad, easy or difficult, we have to live with the results. In the Bible there are a number of stories about people who had to experience consequences because of their actions:

♦ **The three Hebrew youth** found themselves in the fiery furnace because they would not bow down and worship Nebuchadnezzar.

♦ **Daniel** was thrown into the lion's den.

♦ **Paul and Silas** were thrown into prison for preaching the Gospel of Jesus Christ.

♦ **King Saul** lost the anointing of God in his life because he was disobedient to God's will.

♦ **Jonah** was thrown off of a ship and swallowed by a great fish because he decided to go to Joppa when God told him to go to Nineveh to run a revival in that city.

♦ **Saul** of Tarsus was blinded on the road to Damascus because he persecuted Christians.

When a person gambles with their life by smoking, drinking,

67

taking drugs, or indulging in unsafe sex they endanger their health. If you fail to study or learn how to read, write, and count, you will greatly hinder your ability to get a job making a good income because you will not have the basic skills necessary to survive in this world. Every decision that you make in life will affect you in a positive or negative way.

Membership in the Human Race

Regardless of how careful you are and all the precautions you take, uncontrollable experiences will still occur because we are a part of the human race. As members of the human race, we are subject to the errors, judgments, evils, and rules of other people.

The New Testament gospel tells us about the life of Jesus. In these stories about Jesus, one thing is very evident. Jesus was a part of the human race like all of us, and he too was exposed to the evil actions, errors, judgments, jealousies, insecurities, greed, wicked imaginations, and government rules of others.

Jesus was falsely accused, put on trial, and sentenced to death. Some of the people involved in this event were in error; some of them used bad judgment, and some had evil intentions. In general, the people who crucified Jesus were not bad people, but they were a misguided people.

The Jewish leaders were trying to protect what they thought to be the best interests of the Jewish nation. Pontius Pilate, who found no fault in Jesus, was just trying to protect his job. The Roman soldier at the cross was just following the orders. Just like Jesus, who suffered an unjust death at the hands of people, all of us are subject to the actions of humanity. Therefore, suffering is also the result of what other people do or say.

We Are A Part of God's Creation

Everything that occurs in life has a cause and this cause has an effect. This process of cause and effect is evident in every area of life. We see and experience it in the order of God's creation, in human interaction, and in our relationship with God and Christ.

When the conditions are right, volcanic eruptions, tornadoes, earthquakes, tidal waves, monsoons, typhoons and hurricanes exhibit fierce uncontrollable power that will bring massive destruction to anything in its path including people, property, and livestock. These result in suffering, hurt, death, and so on.

During the life span of the human body, if there is an alteration from the biological laws which the human body must live by, it can lead to all kinds of physical problems. Some biological problems we bring upon ourselves or they may be caused by others. Some problems are the result of our environment, and other problems are the result of what some might call Mother Nature's freakish or unfair acts.

Very often we meet people who experience great physical suffering, not because of anything they have done, and we wonder, why did God let that happen? When I was a teenager, I had a good friend by the name of Charlie McWharter. Charlie was a police officer for the city of New York. We met one night after he and his family moved into our neighborhood. On this night I was locked out of my house.

It was a summer night so I knew that the window to my bedroom was open. As I attempted to open and climb through the window to get into my house, Charlie, not knowing me, came over to stop me. After convincing him that this was my home we started talking and developed a really good friendship. Charlie became like a big brother to me.

When I started dating on a regular basis, he would often let me use his car. It was a 1968 maroon, Ford Galaxy 500 with a black vinyl top. On one occasion, he gave me the car for a couple of hours and told me to be back in time for him to be at work at 11:00 that night. On my way home I stopped to put gas in the car and after I did the car would not start. The cause was bad gas from the gas station. Charlie was really upset with me. Yet, after getting the car fixed, he allowed me to use his car again.

Charlie had a lovely family which he took excellent care of. When he and his wife had their second child, they chose me to be her godfather. While in seminary in Atlanta, my mother told me to call Charlie's wife, Fanny, because Charlie had suddenly died.

When I called Fanny, I found out that Charlie had a brain disease that quickly took his life. After talking to her, I walked down Peachtree Street in downtown Atlanta, wondering why such a bad thing happened to such a good man like Charlie McWharter.

One thing is for sure, we like to accept the easy things in God's universe. We accept the pretty days, the warm weather, good health, and people we think look normal or act normal. But the more difficult things in God's creation that make life hard to handle, we will dislike, reject, and avoid as much as we can.

A protégé of Jesus must always remember that rainy days, storms, terminal, diseases, deformities are just as much a part of God's creation as are the easier things to accept. That's why we must stay close to Jesus, live right, and treat others right, because none of us know what the future holds. If we are close to God through our Savior Jesus Christ, we can better handle whatever happens in our lives.

As mankind is allowed to explore the mysteries of God,

man's responsibility to God gets greater. This is extremely important because the more we misuse the powers that God has given us, the more uncontrollable suffering and pain we bring about. The depletion of the ozone layer and the destruction of the rain forest are just a couple of examples.

Four Ways To Demonstrate Your Trust In God

When we consider how fragile we are to our own actions, the actions of others, and the order of the universe, it is easy to see how life can seem unfair to us and out of our control. Demonstrating an unshakable trust in God with the confidence that He is in control requires at least four things.

- Trust and confidence
- Faith in action
- Optimistic attitude
- Knowledge of God's word.

Life's Roller Coaster

In being a protégé of Jesus, the ability to handle life's ups and downs has to be rooted in an attitude of **trust and confidence.** Trust and confidence that God will guide and protect you through every experience in life. In Acts 14:1-19, we can read about one of the many experiences that the apostle Paul had in his ministry. I call this experience a roller coaster experience. Look with me at verse one and verse nineteen:

Verse 1, "And it came to pass in Iconium, that they went both together into the synagogue of the Jews, and so spake, that a great multitude both of Jews and also of the Greeks believed."

Verse 19, "And there came thither certain Jews from Antioch and Iconium, who persuaded the people, and, having stoned Paul, drew him out of the city, supposing he had been dead."

Notice that in the first verse Paul and Barnabus were experiencing a fruitful ministry with people believing the gospel of Jesus and joining the church. But notice in verse nineteen that Paul had been stoned in Lystra and left for dead. When you read the entire 14th chapter of Acts, you will see how the experience of Paul and Barnabus continued a pattern of good and bad, ups and downs.

When you get on the roller coaster at the amusement park, it always travels upward first towards the top. The ride up is usually slow and it gives you an opportunity to see all around the amusement park. If it is a clear and beautiful day, you will be able to see for miles.

Right after that, the roller coaster takes a downward plunge that reaches speeds up to 70 miles per hour. During the ride, you will experience a number of dips, dives, curves, and on some roller coasters you will even go through a few loops.

What I find really interesting is that, when the ride is over, many people will get back in the line again even if the line is long just to do it again. If you ask them why, the most common answer is that it was thrilling. Isn't that interesting? After all a roller coaster ride does to a person, they still will ride it again.

By looking carefully at what motivates people to ride the roller coaster over and over again, you will be able to understand how Paul's confidence in Jesus enabled him to accept the ups and downs in his life. Hopefully, you will understand how an attitude of trust and confidence will help you handle the roller coaster experiences in your life.

A rider on the roller coaster will ride over and over because the rider knows consciously or subconsciously that the owner of the amusement park is committed to the safety of all park visitors. The architects and engineers who design and build the roller coaster build them to be safe by honoring all of the laws of physics and gravity. The operator of the roller coaster is an expert in the operation of the roller coaster and knows just what to do in the case of a crisis.

The apostle Paul was able to ride life's roller coaster because he had an assurance that God would protect him and keep him safe from his enemies. In Acts 18:9-10, the Lord spoke to him and said:

" Be not afraid, but speak, and hold not your peace: For I am with thee, and no man shall set thee to hurt thee: for I have much people in this city." Acts 23:11-25, tells how his nephew overheard a plot to kill him and saved his life.

Paul was able to ride life's roller coaster ride because he knew God as the architect and engineer of the universe, and life itself. Paul was confident that God knew just how much he could bare in His divine plan for Paul's life.

"There hath no temptation taken you but such as is common to man: but God is faithful, who will not suffer you to be tempted above that ye are able; but will with the temptation also make a way to escape, that ye may be able to bear it," 1 Cor 10:13 KJV.

Paul also knew that because God was the operator of life's roller coaster, he could trust the Lord with his life. Paul states in II Timothy 1:12,

"Where unto I am appointed a preacher and an apostle and a teacher of the Gentiles for the which cause I also suffer these; nevertheless I am not ashamed, for I know whom I have believed, and am persuaded that He is able to keep that which I have committed unto him against that day."

Just as confidence and trust allows the rider to enjoy the

thrill of the roller coaster with its high-tech maneuvers, confidence and trust in Jesus Christ allows us to experience the joy of the Lord in the midst of life's ups and downs.

As you experience life's roller coaster with all of its ups and downs, do it with total trust and confidence in God. That's when you will really experience the joy of the Lord which will keep you in peace and contentment because you know that God is in charge.

Let God Be God

After you develop trust and confidence that God is in charge of every situation, then you must put your **faith in action.** As little children, we had no idea of what it took to survive in life. When we had a need to be met, we would confidently turn to our parents, guardian, child care worker, or whoever had charge of our lives.

Growing into young adulthood means taking more responsibility for yourself. As a young adult, you have to handle your own problems and meet your own needs. Whenever you run into a problem that you cannot handle or a concern that bothers you it seems natural to turn to someone who you know and trust to talk to or seek advice. As protégés of Jesus you can turn to God for help in every area of your life, no matter what it is.

Often Christians forget this fact because life is so complicated, and turning to God seems so simple. But when you have a need for direction, when you need guidance out of a messy situation, or when you feel that the pressures of life are about to crush you, turn to God.

Acknowledge God and he will direct you. This applies to your education, career, relationships, finances, anything. If you have made mistakes and are suffering from the consequences, acknowledge God and he will guide you through. You will still have to suffer the consequences, but God will help you through. In other words, turn to God in prayer.

When King David was away from his Kingdom and throne because his son, Absolom started a revolt, turning people against his father, David turned to God in prayer. One such prayer is found in *Psalms 6;*, read it for yourself. When Elisha found himself ready to give up in a cave because he couldn't take the pressures from Queen Jezebel and her husband, King Ahab, he looked for God in the wind and in an earthquake, and in the fire. *I Kings 19.*

When Moses was at the Red Sea with no place to go he sought God in prayer. When Paul and Silas were locked up in prison, they just began to praise God in their situation, *Act 16.* Jonah prayed in the belly of that fish, and Paul prayed about a thorn in his flesh.

As you mature as a Christian, and face more responsibilities, learn how to go to God in prayer for direction. In everything you do in life, turn to God for direction. To do this, you must get into the practice of stopping, listening, and looking up for God's response.

Stop and be still: Stop what you're doing if your actions are contributing to the problem. If the problem is the cause of another action, try to stop antagonizing the situation to the best of your ability. If you can stop and be still, you can avoid more damage or trouble.

An eighteen year old girl once told me about a relationship she had with a young man who was just using her for his personal needs. She said that he was using her to take care of him, his children from another relationship, and sex. She admitted that she was being foolish and that their relationship was stopping her from moving forward with her life. She believed that God was not pleased with her. But when she was asked if she was going to end the relationship, she really did not want to. She was afraid of being alone, and without a man. Fortunately, after another week, she came to her senses and ended the relationship.

Her situation is not unique. I have met a number of people young and old, male and female, who will do unhealthy things to their mind and body, sacrificing their self-worth and dignity to meet the needs of the flesh. As a protégé of Jesus, you do not have to do this. When you find yourself in an unhealthy situation, just stop what you are doing so God can bring you through. The Psalmist wrote:

"God is our refuge and strength, a very present help in trouble. Therefore will not we fear, though the earth be removed, and though the mountains be carried into the midst of the sea; Though the waters thereof roar and be troubled, though the mountains shake with the swelling thereof, Selah.

There is a river, the streams whereof shall make glad the city of God, the holy place of the tabernacles of the most High. God is in the midst of her; she shall not be moved: God shall help her, and that right early. The heathen rage, the kingdoms were moved: he uttered his voice, the earth melted. The Lord of hosts is with us; the God of Jacob is our refuge, Selah.

Come, behold the works of the Lord, what desolation's he hath made in the earth. He maketh wars to cease unto the end of the earth; he breaketh the bow, and cutteth the spear in sunder; he burneth the chariot in the fire.

Be still, and know that I am God: I will be exalted among the heathen, I will be exalted in the earth. The Lord of hosts is with us; the God of Jacob is our refuge, Selah," Psalms 46.

Whenever you get into a situation where you are in trouble and you are in too deep, be still, and pray. Let God be God.

Listen: After you stop doing whatever you were doing, listen and hear what God says to you before you try to solve the problem. Open your heart, mind, and soul to the voice of God. Many times we pray but don't listen for an answer.

Suppose you went to someone for help or advice. After you talked to them, would you wait for their response or would you walk away? Well, that's exactly what we do when we pray and ask God to give us direction and go on about our business without waiting for an answer.

If God doesn't have our attention, how can we hear from Him? So not only do we need to stop what we are doing, we also need to listen for God to speak to us. Taking the time to listen means that we will not be hasty in our action.

Some of you may be asking, how does God speak to people or how will I know when God is speaking? Here are three ways for you to know when God is speaking to you:

1. When God speaks, he will never tell you anything that is contrary to his Word. He will not tell you to lie, cheat, or steal.

2. When God speaks to us, he may speak through a passage of scripture that you may read or hear someone else read. He may speak to you through a song, a sermon, someone's testimony, or prayer.

3. When God Speaks, He will always be direct and to the point and you will feel a personal conviction to honor him with obedience and faith.

In the following passage of scripture, notice how God spoke to Joseph, the father of Jesus and notice what Joseph was doing that made it possible for God to speak to him.

"Now the birth of Jesus Christ was on this wise, When as his mother Mary was espoused to Joseph, before they came

together, she was found with child of the Holy Ghost. Then Joseph her husband, being a just man, and not willing to make her a public example, was minded to put her away privately.

But while he thought on these things, behold, the angel of the Lord appeared unto him in a dream, saying, Joseph, thou son of David, fear not to take unto thee Mary thy wife: for that which is conceived in her is of the Holy Ghost. And she shall bring forth a son, and thou shalt call his name JESUS, for he shall save his people from their sins.

Now all this was done, that it might be fulfilled which was spoken of the Lord by the prophet, saying, Behold, a virgin shall be with child, and shall bring forth a son, and they shall call his name, which being interpreted is, God with us. Then Joseph being raised from sleep did as the angel of the Lord had bidden him, and took unto him his wife," Matthew 1:18-24.

Joseph wasn't hasty in his dealing with Mary. When he found out she was pregnant, he did not respond violently or rashly. Joseph was considerate, passionate, and verse twenty indicates that he gave thought to the situation. It was during this time of meditation, thinking about his problem, and no doubt praying to God, that the angel of the Lord brought him comforting news. Joseph wasn't impulsive; he was thoughtful and slow to act and that gave God an opportunity to speak to him through an angel.

When we are confronted with situations that are out of our control and we turn to God in prayer, we must then be careful to wait on the Lord to hear what the Lord has to say to us. This passage of scripture from the epistle of James explains it well.

"Wherefore my beloved brethren, let every man be swift to hear, slow to speak, slow to wrath: For the wrath of man not the righteousness of God. Therefore lay apart all filthiness and

superfluity of naughtiness, and receive with weakness the engrafted word, which is able to save your souls," James 1:19-21.

Look up and see your victory coming: When things are out of control and you have stopped to listen before you act, then you should look up to God and watch Him do His thing. Nothing is so bad in life that you can't look up to God for deliverance. Don't keep your head down in despair, but look up and see the glory of the Lord. The Psalmist said:

"I will lift up mine eyes unto the hills, from whence cometh my help. My help cometh from the Lord, which made heaven and earth. He will not suffer thy foot to be moved: he that keepeth thee will not slumber. Behold, he that keepeth Israel shall neither slumber nor sleep.

The Lord is thy keeper: the Lord is thy shade upon thy right hand. The sun shall not smite thee by day, or the moon by night. The Lord shall preserve thee from all evil: he shall preserve thy soul. The Lord shall preserve thy going out and thy coming in from this time forth, and even for ever more," Psalms 121.

In 1981, I was traveling from Delaware, Ohio to Xenia, Ohio on state route 42. It was about four o'clock in the morning and the temperature was below zero. Between the towns of London and Cedarville, which are ten miles apart, my car froze up, and I was stranded in the middle of nowhere.

As I stood outside of my car wondering what I would do, I looked up into the clear and cold night sky at the stars that looked like diamonds on a black velvet cloth. I looked to the north and to the south and did not see the lights of any cars coming. As I looked to the east and to the west I knew that I was in the midst of farm land covered with snow.

After a while, a white man driving a new 1981 Buick Riviera

traveling southbound stopped when he saw me standing on the side of the road. After I explained to him my situation, he informed me that there was no police or fire station for me to go to until dawn. So he invited me to go home with him, so I could figure out what I was going to do.

The man told me how his car had been stolen and that he had just gotten it back. He lived in a nice ranch style home. His living room window faced the east. I remember because when the sun came up the crystals of ice on the living room window displayed some beautiful geometric designs.

After talking with this man for about an hour, the man said to me "Russell, take my car and go home. Take care of your business and then come back in a couple of hours and we will get your car going." Because of this, I will always know that God is in control of every situation.

Here was a white farmer who stopped to help me, a black man from New York City. He took me home, then he loaned me his new car he had just gotten back after being stolen. God truly made a way for me when I did not know what to do. By stopping, listening, and looking to God for direction you allow him to act in your life.

What Is Your Outlook on Life?

Along with trust and faith in action, you have to have a positive and optimistic attitude. As a protégé of Jesus you have many good reasons to have an **optimistic attitude** as it relates to your life and your fellowship with Jesus. Allow me to share with you two of these reasons.

One reason is because God's word promises that God will never put on us more than we can handle. The Apostle Paul writes: *"There hat no temptation taken you but such as is common to man: but God is faithful, who will not suffer you to* *be tempted above that yea are able; but will with temptation also make a way to escape, that yea may be able to bear it" I Corinthians 10:13.*

This is a promise that brings a brighter outlook to your life because it says three significant things. First, our own experiences with temptations, tests, and trials are no different than anyone else's. Therefore, we know that we are not alone as we go through life's tests and trials. It also takes away our reason for feeling sorry for ourselves when things get rough. Second, we know that we can handle life's tests and trials that come because God will not put on us more that we can handle. Third, we also know that we will always have a way to escape temptation when it gets too much for us to handle. Jesus says to us in Matthew 11:28 that when our burdens become too heavy we can give them to Him, and He will bear them for us.

The second reason why we should have an optimistic point of view is because things are better than we may think. The apostle Paul wrote: *"Whatsoever things are true, whatsoever things are honest, whatsoever things are just, whatsoever things are lovely, whatsoever things are of good report; if there be any virtue, and if there be any praise, think on these things,"* *Philippians 4:8.*

Focus with me on the portion of this verse that says: *"... whatsoever things are of good report..."* As a protégé of Jesus, I suggest that you develop the following discipline that will cause your outlook on life to be bright everyday.

First, pay attention to the good in every situation rather than focusing on the bad because it will make a difference. When it rains and you notice the silver lining among the dark clouds, or the beautiful rainbow, it will make a difference.

If in the midst of financial suffering, you know that you still have clothes on your back and food in your stomach, it makes a difference. If in the midst of physical sickness, there is still love for life and an effort to live life with joy and peace it will make a difference.

As we look to God for direction in the roller coaster experiences of life, we can always look at the suffering of Jesus and see the good that came out of a bad situation as a source of optimism. Always try to look for the good in every situation.

The author of Hebrews wrote: *"Looking unto Jesus the author and the finisher of our faith; who for the joy that was set before him endured the cross, despising the shame, and is set down at the right hand of God the Father," Hebrews 12:2.*

Second, make it a point to count your blessings on a regular basis. The more you count your blessings, giving thanks to God, the more you will be aware of what God is doing in your life. When you really know what God is doing in your life, it allows you to know and testify to the fact that God is in charge.

"Giving thanks always for all things unto God and the Father in the name of our Lord Jesus Christ," Ephesians 5:20.

I once suggested to a young single mother who was struggling to raise her children in the church with love and dignity, to keep a notebook. In this notebook I told her to list and date each time God blessed her and her children while she was raising them. Then look back over the notebook when her children are grown and count her blessings.

I offer that suggestion to each of you. Try to keep an honest account of your blessings, then look back over your notebook. There will be no way that you will not be able to have the assurance that God is in control.

Last, you will have a better outlook on life if you will forgive yourself and forgive others. Giving and receiving forgiveness has a way of relieving you from the pressures of your guilt, anger, worry, and fear. Forgiveness is a two way process. In order to receive from God, you must give it to others.

Again the words of Paul in his letter to the Ephesians are important to our outlook on life. *"And be ye kind one to another, tenderhearted, forgiving one another, even as God for Christ sakes hath forgiven you," Ephesians 4:32.*

If you ever begin to wonder if God is really in control, begin to think about what God is doing in you, for you, and around you. You will realize that things are better than you think.

You Can Depend On God's Word

As we bring this chapter to an end, consider the following two passages of scripture as a source of assurance that God is in control. Any time you read the Bible, you will find scriptures that will have a special meaning to you. These are two scriptures that I find helpful to me as it relates to my assurance that God is in control. The first passage of scripture comes from Psalms 37;

"Never envy the wicked! Soon they fade away like grass and disappear. Trust in the Lord instead. Be kind and good to others; then you will safely here in the land and prosper, feeding in safety. Be delighted with the Lord. Then he will give you all your heart's desires. Commit everything you do to the Lord.

Trust him to help you do it and he will. Your innocence will be clear to everyone. He will vindicate you with the blazing light of justice shining down as from the noonday sun. Rest in the Lord; wait patiently for him to act.

Don't be envious of evil men who prosper. Stop your anger! Turn off your wrath. Don't fret and worry, it only leads to harm. For the wicked shall be destroyed, but those who trust the Lord shall be given every blessing. Only a little while and the wicked shall disappear. You will look for them in vain.

But all who humble themselves before the Lord shall be given every blessing, and shall have wonderful peace.

The Lord is laughing at those who plot against the godly, for he knows their judgment day is coming. Evil men take aim to slay the poor; they are ready to butcher those who do right. But their swords will be plunged into their own hearts and all their weapons will be broken.

It is better to have little and be godly than to own an evil mans wealth; for the strength of evil men shall be broken, but the Lord takes care of those he has forgiven. Day by day the Lord observes the good deeds done by godly men, and gives them eternal rewards. He cares for them when times are hard; even in famine, they will have enough.

But evil men shall perish. These enemies of God will wither like grass, and disappear like smoke. Evil men borrow and "cannot pay it back!" But the good man returns what he owes with some extra besides. Those blessed by the Lord shall inherit the earth, but those cursed by him shall die."

The steps of good men are directed by the Lord. He delights in each step they take. If they fall it is not fatal for the Lord holds them up with his hand.

I have been young and now I am old. And in all my years I have never seen the Lord forsake a man who loves him; nor have I seen the children of the Godly go hungry. Instead, the godly are able to be generous with their gifts and loans to others, and their children are a blessing.

So if you want an eternal home, leave your evil, low-down ways and live good lives. For the Lord loves justice and fairness; he will never abandon his people. They will be kept safe forever; but all who love wickedness shall perish.

The godly shall be firmly planted in the land, and live

there forever. The godly man is a good counselor because he is just and fair and knows right from wrong.

Evil men spy on the godly, waiting for an excuse to accuse them and then demanding their death. But the Lord will not let these evil men succeed, nor let the godly be condemned when they are brought before the judge.

Don't be impatient for the Lord to act! Keep traveling steadily along his pathway and in due season he will honor you with every blessing, and you will see the wicked destroyed. I myself have seen it happen: a proud and evil man, towering like a cedar of Lebanon, but when I looked again, he was gone!

I searched but could not find him! But the good man— what a different story! For the good man—blameless, the upright, the man of peace—he has a wonderful future ahead of him. For him there is a happy ending. But evil men shall be destroyed, and their posterity shall be cut off.

The Lord saves the godly! He is their salvation and their refuge when trouble comes. Because they trust in him, he helps them and delivers them from the plots of evil men."

Psalms 37, The Living Bible

The second passage comes from Revelations 22:10-14: *"Then he instructed me, Do not seal up what you have written, for the time of fulfillment is near. And when that time comes, all doing wrong will do it more and more; the vile will become more vile; good men will do better; those who are holy will continue on in greater holiness."*

See, I am coming soon, and my reward is with me, to repay everyone according to the deeds he has done. I am the A and the Z, the Beginning and the End, the First and Last. Blessed forever are all who are washing their robes, to have the right to enter in through the gates of the city, and to eat the fruit from the Tree of Life." Revelations 22:10-14, The Living Bible.

In these two scriptures I have found the following truths have helped me to be confident that God is in control and that the Holy Spirit will always lead me and guide me:

1. You do not have to be jealous of anybody who appears to be getting over in a way that is unacceptable to God.
2. If you trust God, He will supply all of your needs.
3. Live according to the will of God, and he will grant you the desires of your heart.
4. In the time of trouble, God also will vindicate you for the world to see.
5. You don't have to exercise vengeance upon your enemies, God will do it in His own time, be patient.
6. Eventually your enemies, those who do you wrong will disappear.
7. Abundant life in God is greater than the "good life" the world offers.
8. Jesus is coming back to set things straight.

I like these truths because whenever things are going wrong and I am affected by the unjust actions of those around me, I can reflect on the promises of God and be content. I offer them to you, in hope that you can relate and have the assurance that you can trust God because he is in control.

Quiz & Discussion

1.   Name the things that cause human pain and suffering.

2.   Name four ways to demonstrate trust in God.

3.   What are three reasons you can trust God on the roller coaster ride of life?

4.   What are three ways to put your faith in action when you turn to God for direction?

5.   Name the three scriptures that support the above three ways.

6.   Name two reasons why a protégé of Jesus should be optimistic.

7.   Name three things you can do to have an attitude of optimism.

Discussion: How does God's Word help you demonstrate trust In God?

Chapter Five

"But ye are a chosen generation, a royal priesthood, an holy nation, a peculiar people; that ye should shew forth praises of him who has called you out of darkness into his marvelous light." I Peter 2:9

Champion - A warrior, fighter; a militant advocate or defender; one who fights for another's right or honor. - Webster's Seventh New Collegiate Dictionary

As a protégé of Jesus you are extremely important to God's plan of salvation for mankind. God wants from your generation young men and women who will be His ambassadors, representing His interests in the world. God needs young people who will be on the cutting edge of Christianity as we move forward and enter a new millennium, making a difference in a world filled with so much trouble.

Since the 1970's the world has seen rapid global changes that have caused shock waves of reality that will be felt in unborn generations to come. One reality is that the world has become more of a global community. What effects one nation can possibly effect another nation instantly. Since the dismantling of the Berlin Wall and the end of the Cold War, the Soviet Union is no longer in existence and communism is apparently on a decline.

Our nation, more specifically the communities across America are becoming more multi-cultural than ever before. Yet racism and prejudice are still fixtures in the American way. The traditional family structure now has many different levels of moral codes and ethical values to choose from that are acceptable in our society.

Another reality is the increasingly destructive nature of gangs in our society. Gangs have always been acceptable in our society. This is evident by our obsession for church denominations, social clubs, fraternities, sororities, and alliances.

In recent years, gangs and drugs have taken a radical turn for the worst. Gangs and drug abuse has adversely affected our society and has made life very difficult in both cities and towns across America.

It is within this global community of change, the body of Christ must again carry the Gospel of our Lord and Savior Jesus Christ into a new millennium: the third millennium since the death and resurrection of Jesus Christ. The charge to go into the world and preach the Gospel has never been as meaningful as it is now.

Because of the technological progress since the days of Jesus, the church has the enormous task of taking the Good News into a world that can completely destroy itself in less than a few hours.

During these two thousand years since the birth of the Christian Church, the Gospel of Jesus Christ that once took the apostles a lifetime to preach in the Middle East, Asia, and Europe, can now travel around the world in less than a few seconds.

This is important because as the years go by, humanity appears to grow distant from God and with the advancement of technology, humankind continues to grow foolish and weaker. The Gospel of Christ must get through to a dying humanity so that every human being can have the opportunity to receive salvation through Jesus Christ in your lifetime.

In the first four chapters, we talked about what it means to be a protégé of Jesus and all of the benefits that come to us. But now I am going to focus on your call to service as a protégé of Jesus. Your call to service can be well defined in the historic and timeless motto of the African Methodist Episcopal Church: "GOD

OUR FATHER, CHRIST OUR REDEEMER AND MAN OUR BROTHER"

As a protégé of Jesus, you are united in Christ with all other Christians to serve God, Christ, and humanity. The apostle Peter said that we are:

A chosen generation: We are a chosen generation because through God's grace we heard and accepted God's Word by faith, accepting Jesus Christ as our Lord and Savior.

A royal priesthood: We are royal because we belong to the family of God. We are a priesthood because we offer sacrifices of praise to God through our worship.

A holy nation, a peculiar people: As a holy nation of believers or protégés of Jesus, we are God's own people, representing Him in the world.

As a protégé of Jesus, you have the responsibility of telling people how God "brought you out of darkness into His marvelous light." As a protégé of Jesus, you are to share the gospel so God's grace will enact faith in non-believers. You are to be an example of God's love and yes, you are to be your brother's keeper.

God is calling for a new generation of soldiers who will raise up in these last days of the twentieth century and be His ambassadors as did the prophets, apostles, and missionaries of times gone by.

What Does God Want You to Do?

The best way to answer this personal question is to look at the ministry of Jesus. When Jesus started his ministry he went to his hometown synagogue and he was given the chance to preach his first sermon. He opened the Bible and read from Isaiah 61 these words.

"The Spirit of the Lord is upon me, because He hath anointed me to preach the gospel to the poor. He hath sent me

to heal the broken hearted, to preach deliverance to the captives, and recovering of sight to the blind. To set at liberty them that are bruised, to preach the acceptable year of the Lord." Luke 4:18-19

When Jesus started his ministry, he did so with five disciples. His ministry consisted of healing, teaching, and pastoral care. One day John the Baptist sent his disciples to Jesus. They asked Jesus, "Are you the one, or shall we look for another?" John wanted to know if Jesus was the Messiah.

Jesus told John's disciples to tell John the things that they heard and have seen. *"The blind receiving their sight, and the lame walking, the lepers are cleansed, and the deaf hear, the dead are raised up, and the poor have the gospel preached to them." Matthew 11:5* From the time of his childhood throughout his ministry Jesus knew what God wanted him to do. He knew that his ministry was one of love and healing.

In a world where there is so much pain and suffering, we are called on to stand on the cutting edge of the Faith with a ministry involving more loving and healing. You do not have to be a preacher, teacher, or doctor to have a ministry of love and healing. Just the right attitude.

Have you ever wondered what Jesus would do if he were physically walking the earth today as He did two thousand years ago? I believe Jesus would go to the most racially troubled spots in the world and would preach deliverance to all who are enslaved by hatred, prejudice, and racism.

I believe that Jesus would meet with the homeless and hungry people world wide, giving them shelter and feeding them fish and bread. I believe that Jesus would go to the hospital wards where the crack babies, addicted babies, and abused babies are and take the time to hold them, love them, and heal them saying, *"suffer little children to come unto me, and forbid them not: for of such is the kingdom of heave," Mark 10:14.*

I believe Jesus would say to the AIDS patients who call on him from outside the walls of social acceptance, "Go to health departments and show yourselves to the doctors. For your faith has made you whole." I believe Jesus would go the dope houses, juke joints, bars, and clubs and spend time with those patrons who wanted to get to see and know him as he did with Zaccheus and the Samaritan woman. I believe Jesus would be as merciful to them as he was to the woman caught in adultery.

Jesus' ministry was one of love and service. As he prepared to leave the earth he told his disciples what he wanted them to do. *"Believe on me and the work I do you shall do better," John 14:12.* What Jesus wants us to do today, one the things that he wanted his disciples to do through the years. We are to take what God has given us and use it to serve God, Christ, and each other. Jesus wants us to be fisherman and ambassadors for Him.

He wants you to be fishers of men, in that, we reach down into the polluted waters of life to rescue the dying and perishing souls. In this world where Satan's kingdom is established, you must stand and say to the world, "Follow me as I follow Christ."

As ambassadors for Christ in this world, you must let the world know that the church is the embassy of God that will stand victoriously until Jesus comes again. It is the refuge place for the fugitives of Satan's kingdom.

As ambassadors your testimony to the world should be, *"For a day in Thy courts is better than a thousand. I had rather be a doorkeeper in the house of my God, than to dwell in the tents of wickedness."* As a champion of God we must courageously represent him in the world just as David represented Israel against Goliath. Just as God made David victorious, he will make you victorious.

There are three things God wants you to do as His champions. First, he wants you to take up a cross. Second, he wants you to stay in His will. Finally, he wants you to stand your ground and say, "devil, you can't steal anything else from me."

Take Up A Cross - *"If any man will come after me let him deny himself and take up his cross and follow me."* Matthew 16:24.

As a protégé of Jesus, you must pick up a cross and carry a load other than yours. Cross bearing is all about ministering to the need of another for Jesus' sake by coming out of the safety, comfort and security zones of our homes and churches.

Jesus didn't have to take the lashes so that by his stripes we would be made whole. Jesus didn't have to shed his blood so we can sing "what can wash away my sins nothing but the blood of Jesus". Cross bearing means voluntarily picking up the burden of others to show them the love of God.

Stay in God's Will - The second thing that God want us to do is stay in His will. Sometimes in bearing the cross, we become weary and are ready to put the cross down. But Jesus teaches us from his experience in the Garden of Gethsemane to say not my will but thy will be done.

When Jesus left the garden of Gethsemane, he was ready to do the Father's will and go to Calvary because of his love for God. Our motivation for doing God's will ought to only be love for God. Jesus said *"if you love me keep my commandments,"* and that is important.

Matthew 7:21, Jesus says *"not everyone that sayeth Lord, Lord shall enter into the kingdom of Heaven, but he that doeth the will of my Father."* Verse 12 reads, *"many will say unto me in that day, Lord didn't we prophecy in your name, didn't we cast out demons in your name, we've done a great work."* Then Jesus will say, *"depart from me ye worker of iniquity, I never knew you," Verse 23.*

After a life of Christian ministry, I don't want to hear the Lord say to me on Judgment Day depart from me worker of iniquity, I don't know you. I want to hear him say, because I stayed in His will, "well done thy good and faithful servant."

Take A Stand

Finally, the Lord wants us to take back from the devil what belongs to us. I share the following story with you because I had to reach a point in my life where I had to take a stand against satan. When I did, Jesus had my back, because I'm a protégé of Jesus.

My Testimony

When I consider the plight of the African-American man, my experiences in growing up in New York, and all of my adventures since I left home, I must proclaim to the world that I have a lot to be thankful for. I am thankful because my experiences in growing up did not involve the degrading extremes of poverty and suffering, and it did not involve the extreme burdens of being ultra rich.

When I reflect over my childhood and upbringing, I am thankful that God allowed me to be a part of an exceptional family. My father did not live at home with us while we were growing up, but he was always nearby. When my sisters and I went to college my father was very supportive and helped us in any way he could. One of the proudest moments for him was visiting me at my first pastoral charge. My proudest moment with my father was when I saw him kneel down at the altar to pray. I had never seen my father pray until that day he came to my church in Pennsylvania. My father died one month later.

Though we did not have a lot of material things, my mother overcame many obstacles through prayer and faith to provide a good home for us. Our home was structured with love, discipline, and a religious value system. We always had a piano to play, books to read, and games to play. We always had family time in which we did things together, ranging from going to the laundry mat, to flying kites in to the park. Because of my mother's faith in God and perseverance my youngest sister is a doctor, my other sister became a corporate attorney, and eventually the City Solicitor of Pittsburg, Pennsylvania, and I am a preacher of the Gospel who God has gifted in many, many ways.

God blessed me with good solid grandparents who were married for almost sixty years. My grandfather was a man of high moral standards, stability, and he had an exceptional mind. My grandmother was a woman of strong determination and religious fervor and she exemplified this character before her children and her grandchildren. God also blessed me with loving and caring aunts and uncles whose influence, patience, support, and memories will forever be in my heart. It was growing up in this kind of family environment through the good times, bad times, and sad times, that made the difference for me as a child and later as an adult.

As children, my sisters and I were reared in the church. I had my first spiritual encounter with God at the age of seven when I attended a revival with my cousin Diana and her husband Emolo. From my Sunday school at Refuge Church of Christ, of the Apostolic Faith in Jamaica, New York I got a good start in understanding the word of God from Bishop Cooper and Elder Charles N. Leader.

At the age of sixteen I became a member of Allen African Methodist Episcopal Church, also in Jamaica, New York. There I was blessed to know progressive people like Reverend and Mrs. Donald Ming who pastored that church when I joined. The Reverend Floyd Flake became pastor of Allen after Rev. Ming was elected the 96th bishops of the A.M.E. Church.

There were a number of people in that great church who taught me a lot and gave me a lot of encouragement.

Because of my involvement in the youth department of Allen, AME Church, I was able to travel around the United States and have many cultural experiences. I was mischievous and sometimes even bad, but I never got in serious trouble as a teenager, at least not to the extent that I was a juvenile delinquent in trouble with the police.

My solid upbringing prepared and helped me to grow up, as well as sustained me away from home when I could have become another tragic statistic among African-American males.

I'm thankful for God's mercy and grace, I left home on September 3, 1973 to attend Wilberforce University in Wilberforce Ohio. A university of the African Methodist Episcopal Church, Wilberforce is the first college in America to be completely owned by African Americans. It was founded in 1857 by Daniel Alexander Payne.

When I left home that day, little did I realize how important my upbringing would be if I was going to be successful and experience the abundant life that Jesus had in store for me. For the next eleven years Satan came at me with every lie imaginable.

At first, he came at me with the works of the flesh and the enjoyments of worldliness. But my greatest obstacle was to overcome the lies I encountered relating to the values I was raised on, relating to marriage, family, ministry, and sex. The works of the flesh and the love of the world were difficult to overcome.

But it was the attack on the mind that did the damage. Satan often used anybody, especially the people I least expected, to misdirect not only me, but many other people too. Sometimes it was very difficult to separate truth from lies. There were many days I found myself walking in spiritual darkness, confused and looking for God to rescue me.

Through all of this I knew that God called me to preach and I knew that I was saved because I repented, confessed, professed, was baptized, and did speak in other tongues. I stayed as close to the body of Christ as I could because I knew that was my only refuge.

Sometimes the salvation experience will dramatically change a person immediately. But sometimes, maybe most of the time, God allows a person to walk in spiritual darkness reaping what he or she sows, but allowing them to evolve into what He wants them to be when they finally yield to His will for their life.

This is a meaningful way to work out your soul salvation, but it is also a difficult and painful way, filled with mistakes, suffering, and needless trials and tribulations along the way. But for some, it may be the only way.

I accepted my call to preach in April of 1974 when Presiding Elder Muldrow licensed me to preach at the New York Annual Conference, held at Allen A.M.E. Church. I had just returned home from Wilberforce University after a deadly tornado ripped through central Ohio leaving a trail of death and disaster.

In October, 1978 I began my ministerial training after I graduated from college. I was admitted into the Ohio Annual Conference of the African Methodist Episcopal Church, in Newark, Ohio. The Presiding Bishop at that time was the Right Reverend Vinton R. Anderson. Bishop Anderson said to me and the other candidates for admission into ministry, *"No man, having put his hand to the plow, and looking back is fit for the kingdom of God." Luke 9:62*

Putting your hand to the plow is a tremendous responsibility that you don't easily get. Many are invited to put their hand to the plow, but many lose the opportunity to do so. Putting your hands to the plow means a complete surrender of self to the will of God and doing things God's way. Without completely surrendering yourself to God's will you are just spinning your wheels and going nowhere fast.

Without full surrender I was jeopardizing the fulfillment of God's purpose in my life and the fulfillment of abundant life in all of its aspects. The truth of the matter is, I had been playing Russian roulette with my enemies, the world, my flesh, and the trickery of the devil.

As I played Russian Roulette, gambling with my mortal body and eternal soul, there were three things given to me by the grace of God that brought me to the point where I was able to finally take my stand against Satan. When I realized this I was able to put my hands to the plow, and realize God's plan for my life.

One was the affect of that strong biblical and moral training I received as a child. The second, was my freedom of choice that God gave me. The third was the protecting hand of God Almighty. I am glad that his grace is sufficient.

It was that biblical and moral training that caused me to be convicted by the call of God's word as I flirted with eternal damnation.

It was also the presence of a loving Savior who heard my prayer for help, forgave me, and received me when I exercised freedom of choice that allowed me to take a stand against my enemies saying, "Enough is enough."

The final thing that God gave me while I was playing Russian roulette was "Divine Protection." God in His mercy and grace kept me safe and sound from physical devastation and death. I believe that every time I hung out in the valley of the shadow of death, truly He was there with His rod and staff, exercising great patience. I thank you Lord Jesus!!!

When I think about my life and God's will for my life and how I jeopardized it, I am thankful for God's word found in the

8th chapter of Romans.

"And we know that all things work together for the good of them that love the Lord who are called according to his purpose. For whom he did foreknow, he also did predestinate to be conformed to the image of his Son, that he might be the first born among many brethren. Moreover whom he did predestinate, them he also called, them he justified, them he also glorified. What shall we then say to these things? If God before us, who can be against us" Romans 8:28-31.

While I walked in spiritual darkness with God's Word convicting me, I was reaping what I sowed. My life was full of pain and misery, and the joys of abundant life were out of my reach. But I am thankful that God had a plan and a purpose for my life long before I came into existence, contingent upon the choices I made.

When God's grace came to me in the form of His Word, calling me from sin to repentance and salvation I found Jesus waiting patiently for me to truly recognize Him as my Savior, Friend, and Lord.

When I think of how I was given hope, deliverance, and victory, I am overwhelmed that Jesus loved me enough to take a personal interest in me. So I can relate to the sixteenth century testimony of Charles Wesley in his hymn, *"And Can It Be That I Should Gain"* I always knew that the Lord loved me. But when I took a stand against the devil I found out how much the Lord loved me.

If you are serious about working for God, fulfilling your purpose in life and experiencing abundant life you are going have to say in the name of Jesus, "Satan, back off, enough is enough." Don't let him get the best of you and your life. Remember, in your service to God, be willing to take up a cross, stay in the will of God, and take a stand against the enemy.

Weapons For Battle

In the second chapter we told you that God provides us with everything we need to overcome anything. Paul refers to the weapons of faith as the *"Whole Armor Of God,"* which comes from Isaiah chapter 59:16-17. In Paul's letter to the Ephesians, he used Isaiah's illustration to describe the armor and weaponry of a soldier.

In order for you, me, or anyone to take up a cross, stay in the will of God, and take a stand against Satan, we must be equipped for the battle. If we are not equipped for battle, Satan will be able to lie to us, rob us, and destroy us. Read what Paul said to the Ephesians church about the necessity for the "Whole Armor Of God."

"Finally, my brethren, be strong in the Lord and in the power of his might. Put on the whole armor of God, that ye are able to stand against the wiles (trickery) of the devil. For we wrestle not against flesh and blood, but principalities, against powers, against rulers of the darkness of this world, against spiritual wickedness in high places. Wherefore take unto you the whole armor of God, that you may withstand the evil day, and having done all, to stand. Stand therefore, having your loins (body) gritted (tied) about with truth, and having on the breastplate of righteousness; and your feet shod (covered in the form of a shoe) with the preparation of the Gospel of peace;

Above all, taking the shield of faith, wherewith ye shall be able to quench all the fiery darts of the wicked. And take the helmet of salvation, and the sword of the spirit, which is the word of God," Ephesians 6:10-17.

The symbolism of the whole armor of God illustrates what it takes to be an effective champion for God. Let me just suggest to you how Paul's illustration of the whole armor of God can relate to you.

As a champion for God, you need the breastplate of righteousness (God's approval that comes only through Jesus Christ) to keep you standing alert against the attacks of the enemy. (The world, our flesh, and the deceitful act and words of the devil)

You need to wear truth like a strong belt on your body that holds up your strong conviction in the teachings of Jesus Christ. You must wear the Gospel of peace like shoes that can and will go anywhere with the Good News of Jesus. The shield of faith represents your forward progress with complete confidence and trust in God.

Finally, your helmet of Salvation represents your divine protection and God's love, interest and concerns for a dying world is represented by the sword of the Spirit which is the Word of God.

Standing On The Cutting Edge

As God's champion standing on the cutting edge of the faith, you must make a difference in your home, your community, and your overall environment.

You must boldly stand, lifting up the blood-stained banner of Christ Jesus by letting your light shine for Jesus so the sin-sick, lost, and broken-hearted can find peace. Be a protégé for Jesus.

Quiz & Discussion

1. According to the Apostle Peter all Christians are what?

2. Where can that be found in the Bible?

3. What does God want you to do?

4. According to the apostle Paul, what is the name of our weapon for battle?

5. What scripture can you find Paul's discussion about our weapon for battle?

6. What scripture in the Old Testament did Paul get his reference about our weapon for battle?

7. What does our weapon for battle consist of?

Discussion: What can Christian youth do to make a difference in their homes, churches, schools, and communities?

Conclusion

A Message of Hope, Deliverance, and Victory

Traveling on the road of life is like traveling on the highway systems of America from one place to another. As you travel, you will see the countryside revealing the handiwork of God. You will see those purple mountains with their majesty across the fruited plains. You will see the great cities built by man. You will see beautiful trees that have been standing for over one hundred years. You will see the desert, the Great Plains, the oceans, rivers, canyons, rolling hills, and much of the beauty of this earth.

As you travel the road of life you will see the beauty of life. You will recognize the beauty of your life, your potential, your dreams, and your aspirations. You will know that your future is promising. But in life's beauty there are still some realities that you must accept. When you travel on the highway systems of America, you will experience storm clouds, rainstorms, windstorms, snowstorms, floods, and blizzards.

I will never forget the time my family and I were traveling through Missouri on Interstate 55 north. We noticed the clouds were dark and low. But our spirits were lifted when we noticed rays of sunlight piercing through those dark clouds making beautiful sunbeams that fell to the earth, lighting a path through the darkness. It was beautiful. For the rest of that trip, Elaine, Chastidy, Audrey, and I sang: *A Sun Beam, a Sun Beam, Jesus wants me for a Sun Beam. A Sun Beam, a Sun Beam, I'll be a Sun Beam for Him.*

Protégé

As you travel life's highway, things may look good to you. You may feel really good and think that you can conquer the world, but eventually you will experience some troubled times and some serious storms. Some of these storms you will bring on yourself, others will be the result of your humanity. Some will occur just because you are God's creation. Some of you may have been depressed in the past. Some of you may be depressed right now and feel that things are going very badly in your life. The beauty of life may seem like a distant dream to you. Whatever your situation may be, always remember, God will break through the storm clouds in your life with a ray of light for your path, a sun beam.

God's Word will reveal a truth to you that will set you free. His Word will give you a message of Hope, Deliverance, and Victory. God wants you to know for yourself that Jesus Christ is truly the answer for the world and for your life. I'm thankful to God that I personally know Him for myself and can share with you from my relationship with God. If you are looking for help, love, identity, and a future, Christ has a lot to offer you. If you feel trapped by bad habits, peer pressure, depression, or even an attitude of hatred, Jesus Christ will help you to overcome these things. God fixed it that the quality of your life is based on the choices you make and the things you do. No matter what you experience in life, God is in control and will guide you through life, if you trust Him. Last, if you think your life has little value or is filled with mistakes, God still has a special purpose for you.

So be a Protégé of Jesus.

NOTES

Main Street Publishing, Inc.
206 E. Main Street Suite 207

Mailing Address:
P.O.Box 696
Jackson, Tn 38302

Toll Free #: 866-457-7379
or
Local #: 731-427-7379

Visit us on the web:
www.mainstreetpublishing.com
www.mspbooks.com